**The Ivory and
Ebony Towers**

The Ivory and Ebony Towers

**Race Relations
and Higher Education**

Charles Vert Willie ,1927-
Harvard University"

LexingtonBooks
D.C. Heath and Company
Lexington, Massachusetts
Toronto

Library of Congress Cataloging in Publication Data

Willie, Charles Vert, 1927-
    The ivory and ebony towers.

    1. College integration—United States. 2. Universities and colleges—
United States—Students. I. Title.
LC214.2.W535   378.73   80-8946
ISBN 0-669-04479-2   AACR2

Published simultaneously in Canada

Printed in the United States of America

International Standard Book Number: 0-669-04479-2

Library of Congress Catalog Card Number: 80-8946

Contents

Contents

List of Tables

Preface and Acknowledgments

This book is a comparative analysis of the adaptations of black and of white students to each other and to their teachers and administrators in institutions of higher education. Complementarity is the basic theme. Examples demonstrate the principle that the majority population that is educated in a setting that excludes the minority receives a deficient education, and vice versa.

How do different populations serve each other when they interact as equals? What can whites learn from blacks? What can blacks learn from whites? This book provides an extensive analysis of the educational value of diversity in learning environments and of the benefits of the minority status. In addition, it reports on the knowledge and wisdom derived from the white experience as a minority on predominantly black college campuses as well as the black experience as a minority on predominantly white college campuses.

An educational philosophy is discussed that emphasizes adequacy rather than excellence as an institutional requirement. Other institutional issues such as the moral and ethical responsibility of colleges and universities in the community are considered. Excellence is identified as a personal goal to which one may aspire, but not as an achievement that institutions should demand of its participants.

Education as liberation versus education as indoctrination is analyzed, and the contributions of black and white populations to these two orientations are examined. The curriculum, including courses such as black studies, language usage, labels, other symbols, and patterns of participation in campus organizations are identified as ways that institutions of higher education may exclude and discriminate or include and liberate.

The discussion in various chapters is critical of some studies of higher education such as one that mislabeled most black colleges as academic disaster areas, and it is complimentary of the extraordinary effort of some small colleges, white and black, which have specialized in teaching and, consequently, developed outstanding individuals such as Dan Rather, a television news specialist, and Martin Luther King, Jr., whom Hugh Gloster of Morehouse College called the archetype of an educated person, worthy of emulation by all.

A new perspective of the function and future of predominantly black colleges includes a description of the contributions that these colleges have made to the higher education system of the nation. This study gives reasons why some blacks enroll in predominantly white schools and why some whites enroll in predominantly black schools. The quality of life for blacks and whites on campuses in which each group is a minority is examined. The quality of the faculty in terms of academic credentials and cosmopolitan experience in predominantly white and in predominantly black institutions is also investigated.

This book is intended as a contribution toward clarifying a philosophy of higher education, increasing the understanding of school desegregation, and adding to the knowledge of the theory and practice of race relations. The analytical perspective is sociological and emphasizes situational sociology as it applies to dominant and subdominant power groups.

The author is most grateful to the Spencer Foundation for providing a grant that supported the preparation of this book. The Foundation and its president, H. Thomas James, responded cheerfully to all requests for resources to initiate and complete this project. Others who assisted in various aspects of the project were Susan L. Greenblatt, Paul Schnider, and Betty Blake. Editorial assistance was rendered with care and concern by Katherine O. Parker. And, of course, I was nurtured and sustained while walking through the lonesome valley of research and writing by my family—Mary Sue, Sarah, Martin, and James.

Gregory Kannerstine, senior coauthor of "Characteristics of Faculties in Predominantly White and Predominantly Black College Campuses," generously gave his permission to reprint this chapter. Thanks also are extended to Parameter Press of Wakefield, Massachusetts for permission to publish "Living In, Between, and Beyond the Races," and to Praeger Publishers for permission to reprint "Recruitment and Financial Aid" and "Black Studies," written by myself and Arline McCord.

The ideas presented in this book are tempered by more than one-third of a century of experience as a student, teacher, or administrator in predominantly black and predominantly white institutions of higher education in both southern and northern regions of the United States.

Part I
Philosophy of Education: Goal, Purpose, Method

1 Inclusiveness: A Philosophy of Education Derived from the Black Experience

Increasing numbers of high-school graduates are receiving college educations. Among the more rapidly growing sectors of higher education today are two-year colleges and predominantly black colleges. Of the millions of students enrolled in higher education today, one-third or more matriculate from two-year colleges. Predominantly black institutions of higher education have increased the size of their student bodies by a factor of more than four since the U.S. Supreme Court *Brown* decision in 1954.

The lifetime average income of individuals is significantly related to education and may have something to do with the enlarged population in colleges and universities. A college education makes a difference in one's earning capacity. The U.S. Bureau of the Census reported that just four or more years of schooling beyond high school can increase average lifetime income to a sum that is more than 50 percent larger than what it would be if one leveled off at high school (1978, p. 131-172). These facts indicate that more and more people will enroll in postsecondary educational institutions in the years to come because the major source of income for most people in the United States is wages.

Beyond economic benefits, blacks and other minorities have tended to look upon education as a means of liberation. Material wealth may be expropriated, but knowledge and wisdom endure.

Adequacy versus Excellence

The most radical change that is likely to occur in higher education in the future, partly because of the increased numbers of participants, is a shift in goals from an institutional requirement of excellence to a cultivation of adequacy. Individuals may aspire to be excellent, but society and its institutions have the right to require only that its members be adequate. The requirement of excellence can contribute to the exclusion of some individuals who can perform in an adequate way to make a real contribution to the welfare of others.

Excellence is fine and beautiful. But adequacy is good enough. Adequacy, however, is not synonymous with mediocrity. Adequacy and inadequacy are of social concern. A society has a right to expect that the persons to whom its members turn are good enough possibly to help and certainly not to harm them. Such are adequate persons. Extraordinary skill beyond the capacity to help and not harm are found in those who are excellent. We tend to esteem excellence. But there is a danger that excellence in one area may be achieved at the expense of adequacy in several other areas. Thus, aspiration for excellence should be weighed and considered in the light of a balanced life. The admissions policy of many black colleges is based on the principle that adequacy is good enough (Willie and MacLeish 1976, p. 92-100). These institutions are inclusive. They are reluctant to exclude, which institutions tend to do when they strive for excellence.

Adequacy does not result in defective outcomes and ineffective functioning. Adequacy denotes that which is equal to or sufficient for a specific requirement. Who could ask for a better outcome of education than that it prepare people to be equal to or sufficient for their tasks and responsibilities? It does not matter how many people are educated as long as they are prepared to function in an adequate way. Indeed, it is probable that when many in society are adequate there is less need for a few who are excellent or extraordinary.

Some will have difficulty dealing with this development in higher education because they are committed to ideas of the nineteenth century that justify excluding all except the best. "The idea of competition, natural selection, and the survival of the fittest" is one of six leading ideas from this period that dominate the minds of educated people today, according to E.F. Schumacher (1973, p. 88). This idea is manifested in the writings of Daniel Bell, who declared that "the post-industrial society, in its initial logic, is a meritocracy. Differential status and differential income are based on technical skills and higher education. Without those achievements one cannot fulfill the requirements of the new social division of labor which is a feature of that society." Bell proclaimed that "in the nature of meritocracy, as it has been traditionally conceived, what is central to the assessment of a person is the assumed relation of achievement to intelligence." Asserting that the number of talented persons in a society as measured by I.Q., is a limited pool, Bell stated that "by the logic of a meritocracy, these high-scoring individuals, no matter where they are in society, should be brought to the top in order to make the best use of their talents" (1977, pp. 607-608).

Some educators, such as those in predominantly black colleges, have questioned this concept and doubted its validity. Judson Jerome asked, "Why is the academy so preoccupied with 'standards,' a word implying conformity on the one hand and hierarchy on the other?" He blamed the Puritan ethic, to which many subscribe, for placing a value on achievement that is so high "that we destroy one another in our disappointment with ourselves and vicious judgments of others." He accused colleges and universities of recruiting for the elite. Jerome raised what he called the most basic question: "Has a college any more right to choose whom it will educate than a barber to decide whose hair he will cut, than a restaurant to decide whom it will serve, than a landlord to decide whom he will house?'' (1971, p. 96).

Jerome described the selective process in U.S. colleges as one way of reinforcing the class structure. His observations of special education teachers and how they relate to handicapped students caused him to believe that the selective process may be important in reinforcing social stratification but has little to do with education. A quality of the special education teachers that all educators should cultivate, according to Jerome, is the capacity to automatically accept students. Special education teachers ''are pleased at progress and do not punish failure.'' They recognize that they are dealing with a wide variety of individuals with different patterns and rates of learning. They assume that their mission is one of assisting growth and development, and that if a child is not interested, not engaged, not learning, the staff needs to reexamine itself and the program (Jerome 1971, pp. 24, 36, 105-106, 224). Because of this approach to education, special education teachers have helped all sorts and conditions of people to learn. Without being accepted as they are, handicapped students would have been sorted out of the formal educational system and left behind in favor of those who can perform in an excellent way.

A society in which many are educated and qualified as adequate is likely to be a self-correcting society. There is little accountability where only a few are excellent, preeminent, and extraordinary—especially if such persons are turned to as the final decision makers. Edward Jenner is credited with developing the vaccine against smallpox. This brilliant scientist was able to accomplish his goal only because of the testimony of a milkmaid who was a sufficiently astute observer to inform the physician that people exposed to cowpox seemed not to get smallpox. Jenner listened to the milkmaid, conducted his experiment, confirmed the relationship between the two diseases, and developed an effective vaccine (Williams 1959, pp. 16-44). A society that deliberately cultivates many astute, adequate observers is better capable of solving its problems than a society in which only a few are trained to be excellent.

It is difficult to understand this principle when education is thought of as a product for personal gain rather than as an exchange process for the public good. Conceived of as a product, education is exhaustible and the quality-quantity argument is applicable. We know that an increase in the quantity of a commodity is likely to result in a decrease in its quality. Education is not a commodity, a phenomenon of exhaustible supply, because by its nature education results from an exchange process. The more people who participate in education the better it is.

In this respect, education is like health and cannot be hoarded. The health of a few individuals is jeopardized by the diseases of many

individuals. Health, therefore, is a public benefit that enhances one individual to the extent that it enhances others. With reference to health and
education, quantity enhances quality and does not diminish it. By achieving
universal education at the elementary and secondary levels, and by increasing the number of individuals to whom educational opportunities are
available at the college and university level, formal schooling is pointing
toward a future of lifelong learning for the many rather than for a few.
Such learning processes will equip individuals to be adequate, that is, equal
to the situations in which they find themselves and sufficiently trained to
fulfill the requirements of society.

Ultimately, such an education is better for the individual as well as for
society. Higher education that prepares for adequacy enables one not only
to pursue a specialty but also to understand how that specialty is linked to
other pursuits. Schumacher commented upon this issue in his book *Small Is
Beautiful:* "All subjects, no matter how specialized, are connected in a
center; they are like rays emanating from a sun. The center is constituted by
our most basic convictions, by those ideas which really have the power to
move us. In other words, the center consists of metaphysics and ethics, of
ideas that—whether we like it or not—transcend the world of facts." Then
Schumacher proclaimed that "the truly educated [person] is not [one] who
knows a bit of everything" but one who is "truly in touch with the center"
(1973, pp. 94-95).

In our striving for excellence and preeminence, we overcome the distrac-
tions of divergence by a process of reductionism wherein all that we do is
significant only if it can be transformed into a convergent process that contributes to the solution of the problems of our specialties. A process that
channels all that we do in one direction for the purpose of attaining
preeminence and excellence can result in the loss of an understanding of
"all higher forces to enable human life and the degradation not only of the
emotional part of our nature but also . . . of our intellect and moral
character." Schumacher said that "the true problems of living . . . are
always problems of overcoming or reconciling opposites. . . . They demand . . . not merely the employment of reasoning power but the commitment of [one's] whole personality" (1973, p. 98).

Quite possibly the striving for excellence and preeminence is a spurious
solution to the problem of divergence. This approach deals with diversity by
eliminating and excluding the less worthy. The widespread development of
adequacy might be more appropriate because this approach is inclusive.
Higher education is moving in this direction. It would appear to be appropriate for all individuals to be taken seriously and to be treated as worthy and for education not to be limited to a few. Such an approach to higher
education in a democracy will develop a polymorphic population and
recognizes the principle articulated so well by the Canadian writer

Robertson Davies that when we commit ourselves to others, we neglect them at our peril (1976, p. 288). In the United States, we have committed ourselves to diversity. We ignore any of the populations in our pluralistic society at our own peril.

Double Culture, Double Consciousness, and Double Victory

Higher education concerned with the development of adequate students will focus less and less on exclusiveness and more on maintaining within the institution a double culture, helping students develop a double consciousness, and teaching students to seek a double victory. The goals of higher education, which are so appropriate for a pluralistic nation, have emerged largely out of the black experience.

The ghetto existence for blacks in the past has been a living example of the double culture, of attaining unity out of diversity. Residential segregation by social class, characteristic of the society at large, has not been fully duplicated in the black community. Affluent and poor blacks live near each other, talk among themselves, and become friends. The continuous dialogue and association between the high and mighty and the meek and lowly in the black ghetto have resulted in genuine communication and caring across the social classes.

The black college campus that draws its students from the black communities of this nation is a reflection of the diversity of these communities. Thus, black college campuses consist of the poor and the affluent—the dispossessed and the well connected. Such diversity provides an inhospitable environment for the development of social class stereotypes. Black students know that ability is more or less randomly distributed in the population and that limited opportunity often is manifested in limited achievement until teachers and students together find ways of overcoming the impediments of the past. They know this because they see on a daily basis students from impoverished backgrounds becoming scholars and leaders on campus. Affluent black students can understand the point of view of poor black students, and vice versa, because the person who has experienced socioeconomic opportunities that are different from one's own frequently is a friend—a classmate, possibly a roommate.

Interaction among students of varying socioeconomic circumstances on the black college campus has enriched these students' knowledge and understanding of a wider range of human nature. Such an education is different from that obtained indirectly about people whom one has not seen and does not know by name. Thus, the coming together of all types of students on the black college campus is a pedagogical as well as a humanistic experience recommended for all learning environments. Majority as well as minority populations will benefit from experiencing socioeconomic diversity.

The requirement for the future for all colleges and universities is that they continue to recruit student bodies, faculties, and administrative staffs that are diversified racially and socioeconomically as well as in other background characteristics. A campus of diversity is an example of the double culture that is inclusive.

The concept of double consciousness has been explored by social scientists such as Charles Horton Cooley (1902, p. 152), who wrote about the "looking-glass self" in which one tries to see oneself as others see one, and George Herbert Mead (1934, p. 175), who conceptualized the self as consisting of the "I" (the affirmation of being) and the "me" (the confirmation of being). In race relations W.E.B. DuBois had this to say about the double consciousness:

> The Negro is a sort of seventh son, born with a veil, and gifted with second-sight in this American world—a world which yields him no true self-consciousness, but only lets him see himself through the revelation of the other world. It is a peculiar sensation, this double consciousness, this sense of always looking at one's soul by the tape of a world that looks on in amused contempt and pity. One ever feels his two-ness—an American, a Negro; two souls, two thoughts, two unreconciled strivings; two warring ideals in one dark body, whose dogged strength alone keeps it from being torn asunder.

> The history of the American Negro is the history of this strife—this longing to attain self-conscious manhood, to merge his double self into a better and truer self. In this merging he wishes neither of the older selves to be lost. He would not Africanize America, for America has too much to teach the world and Africa. He would not bleach his Negro soul in a blood of white Americanism for he knows that Negro blood has a message for the world: He simply wishes to make it possible for a man to be both a Negro and an American (1903a, p. 13-14).

Although DuBois spoke of blacks in the United States, it is clear that he saw the minority or subdominant status in a common culture as the source of double consciousness that is inclusive. It is fair to say that double consciousness is a property of being a member of the less powerful group. This status requires the examination of one's role from the perspective of others as a means of survival. Persons with limited resources must outmaneuver those who are more powerful if the powerful are not compassionate.

The responsibilities of minorities and majorities or dominant and subdominant people of power are quite different. As minorities in the United States, blacks, and particularly black students in black colleges, have insisted that this nation live up to its principles and fulfill its laws pertaining to freedom and justice. However, no society ever functions properly if run only according to law. Generosity is possible only among people who control resources. No one is required to give more than his or her fair share. Yet a society cannot operate effectively unless some are generous and give more than they are required to give. The dominant people of power who control community resources must learn to be generous. This is one of their essential responsibilities. They can practice generosity only in the presence of people of lesser resources. Majorities, therefore, need minorities if they would learn to be generous.

Likewise, a society cannot function effectively without some people who are willing to give up their fair share and take less than they are entitled to receive. This magnanimous activity is often seen among minorities or the subdominant people of power. For years, blacks have made do with few of the resources of this land, have persevered, and have overcome. Their loyalty to a nation that has treated them unjustly for several centuries attests to their magnanimity—an action that is possible only among those who are not in charge.

Because all at varying times and in different situations may be members of the minority and of the majority, it is important to learn how to adapt to the requirements of both positions and to fulfill their required roles. Blacks who seldom have been in control need to learn how to be genuinely generous. Whites who seldom have acknowledged their dependency on others need to learn the responsibilities of magnanimity.

Double consciousness enables the minorities to see themselves as they are seen by the majority. It is well that members of a majority population become a minority population at some period during their education so that they can better understand themselves through the development of a dual perspective. Also, it is of value that all minorities should become the majority at some period in their education so that they may understand the essential contribution of the majority to human society. Black colleges have helped minorities develop a double consciousness. Now it is time for them to help whites develop a double consciousness by living as a minoritiy, an idea that will be discussed in greater detail in chapter 3. They can help the majority by making it possible for members of the majority to become the minority in predominantly black colleges, for double consciousness is a property of subdominant power groups.

A college education for blacks never has been a self-centered thing, even though it has been achieved for the purpose of helping oneself as well as others. Blacks have been taught in their institutions that the greatest of all is first the servant of all. Always they have been advised that personal success is of limited advantage if it does not contribute to the uplifting of the race. This message can be generalized. In seeking the uplifting of their own race, blacks must at the same time seek the uplifting of whites. Essentially, this is the message that characterized the civil rights movement led by Martin Luther King, Jr. In seeking victory for the individual, one has to seek victory for the group, and in seeking victory for the oppressed group, one has to seek victory for those who formerly were the oppressors. The inclusive approach is what King called the double victory. Blacks, and particularly black college students, in their peaceful demonstrations subordinated individual success to group advancement. This orientation was most clearly manifested during the civil rights demonstrations of the 1960s when students risked their college careers to picket in behalf of their less educated friends and family members. Getting ahead personally by putting down others has not been the way of life of black college students.

The double victory is achieved when there is mutual fulfillment. There is no victor and vanquished but a synthesis that consists of the old parts related to each other in a new way. Thus, the justice that blacks seek is a justice for whites as well as for blacks. The freedom that blacks seek is a freedom for minorities as well as the majority. The truth that blacks seek cannot be limited to any race. In the past, blacks sought a double victory in education that uplifted the individual as well as the group. Now blacks can demonstrate how the double victory in education uplifts whites as well as blacks.

Already black colleges have made a contribution to higher education in the United States by keeping alive in their students knowledge and understanding of the double culture, the double consciousness, and the double victory. They now must extend their missions beyond immersion in the dual condition of affluence and poverty to include interaction between white and black students. They now must go beyond the development of a double consciousness in which minorities see themselves from the point of view of the majority, and also help the majority see itself from the point of view of minorities. They must no longer be satisfied with helping individual blacks find fulfillment and with helping all blacks; liberated blacks now must help free whites. Such is the double victory.

Beyond the concepts of double culture, double consciousness, and double victory, blacks in higher education have made a major contribution to resolving the tension between other dualities such as career and classical education. The debate between two black educators—Booker T. Washington and W.E.B. DuBois—helped the nation understand how these two orientations in higher education could coexist and complement each other.

Classical and Career Education

In *Culture out of Anarchy: The Reconstruction of American Higher Learning,* Judson Jerome told about Antioch's Inner College, with which he was affiliated at the time. One focus of activity at the Inner College for men and women students was "baking bread" (Jerome 1971, p. 266). Jerome noted approvingly that some young people in college had turned their attention to learning how to survive. Literally, their education was in the "hard subject of providing heat and food for themselves, making do with almost no . . . convenience" (1971, p. 266). Such educational experiences had been fashioned, he said, because "young people have a genuine desire to rediscover their hands." The twentieth century was two-thirds spent before some colleges and universities recognized this desire in the young who came to them for an education.

Black educators recognized this desire decades earlier, at the beginning of this century. In 1903, Booker T. Washington said "that the very best service which any one can render to what is called the higher education is to teach the present generation to provide a material . . . foundation." Elaborating on this point, he said: "I have been discouraged as I have gone through the South . . . and have found [people] who could converse intelligently upon abtruse subjects, and yet could not tell how to improve the condition of the poorly cooked . . . bread . . . which they and their families were eating three times a day" (Washington 1903, p. 224). Washington called learning to work with one's hands industrial education. He defended it as a legitimate form of education that consists of teaching one "how to make the forces of nature . . . work for [one]." He concluded that if industrial education (that is, rediscovering one's hands and learning how to provide heat, food, and other essentials) has any value, "it is in lifting labor up out of toil and drudgery into the plane of the dignified and the beautiful" (1903, p. 225).

Jerome endorsed this pragmatic orientation and the search for relevance found among students in contemporary times. However, he looked to "liberal education [to] enlarge . . . a narrow pragmatic orientation toward education and human worth." Liberal education, he said, "has something to do with the definition of [men and women], with [their] unique awareness of [their] own mortality, [their] capacity for reflection, for holding the future and past along with the present in [their] mind[s]" (Jerome 1971, p. 275).

It took the student uprisings of the 1960s to bring Jerome and other educators to their senses about the multiple functions of liberal education to deal with the pragmatic as well as the philosophical, and the collective as well as the individual. Yet in 1903, William E.B. DuBois wrote that "it is the [person] and not the material product, that is the true object of education" (1903b, p. 227). He defined education as "that whole system of human training within and without school house walls, which molds and develops [people]" (1903b, p. 226). DuBois drew attention to the "street academy" and the "university without walls" decades before they were fashionable and faddish. The development of the mind, for him, was a continuous process not limited to any place or any age category.

Moreover, DuBois saw moral education as an essential component of higher education: "Education must not simply teach work—it must teach life" (1903b, p. 228). For DuBois, education had the threefold function of strengthening character, increasing knowledge, and teaching one how to earn a living. DuBois admitted that it was hard to do all of these simultaneously. But he said, resolutely, "It will not do to give all the attention to one and neglect the others" (1903b, p. 226).

Had Jerome and other educators learned the wisdom of DuBois, they would have recognized early on that pragmatic and philosophical orientations complement each other in higher education, that a dollar sign and a job can be one motivation for obtaining more schooling, and that learning how to promote justice can simultaneously be an objective of higher education.

Commenting upon the interrelationships between knowledge and character, and character and work, DuBois, said, "We might simply increase [one's] knowledge of the world, but this would not necessarily make one wish to use this knowledge honestly; we might seek to strengthen character and purpose, but to what end if . . . people have nothing to eat or to wear" (1903b, p. 226).

Both DuBois and Washington were influenced by their debate. Washington finally conceded that training of the hands without mental training as well is a crude kind of training for selfish purposes and is inappropriate (1903, p. 223). DuBois admitted that the teaching of work is an important function of education. Indeed, he called it "the paramount necessity." But then he said, "Work alone will not do . . . unless inspired by the right ideals and guided by intelligence" (DuBois 1903b, pp. 227-228). The essential difference between Booker T. Washington and W.E.B. DuBois was not educational but political, involving strategy and tactics for race relations and social change. They wrestled with the idea of education and achieved a consensus that the pragmatic and the theoretical go hand in hand. Their understanding of higher education was ignored by other educators in the nation. It was during the 1950s that a learned professor would write: "If a college is to produce educated [people], it should concern itself with both liberal and practical education" (Jerome 1971, p. 264). Such an affirmation is based on the foundation of the Washington-DuBois debate a half century earlier, which was not acknowledged as the intellectual heritage of a "new" understanding.

Why did it take the leaders of American higher education so long to deal with the issues raised in the Washington-DuBois debate? The answer I derive is racism. White America ignored the Washington-DuBois debate as two blacks fussing with each other, making "much ado about nothing."

White America did not realize that the issues with which these men were wrestling were central to the education of all people. We must not commit this error again and ignore the initiatives of black educators and black schools. America has much to learn from the black experience.

Archetype of an Educated Person

Martin Luther King, Jr. is a magnificent manifestation of the black experience in America. A decade after his death, Hugh Gloster of Morehouse College called him the archetype of an educated person—one who combined academic achievement and professional success with personal integrity and social concern. He said that the life of Martin Luther King, Jr. was worthy of emulation by all (*Morehouse College Bulletin* 1980, 5).

Education for adequacy is compatible with an education that emphasizes the double culture, double consciousness, and a double victory. Education for adequacy is the contribution of the black experience to the emerging American philosophy of education of inclusiveness.

References

Bell, Daniel, 1973. "On Meritocracy and Equality." In *Power and Ideology in Education,* edited by Jerome Karabel and A. H. Halsey, pp. 607-635. New York: Oxford University Press.

Brown v. *Board of Education of Topeka.* 1954. 347 U.S. 483.

Cooley, Charles Horton. 1902. *Human Nature and the Social Order.* New York: Scribner's.

Davies, Robertson. 1976. *The Manticore.* New York: Penguin Books.

DuBois, W.E.B. 1903a. "Our Spiritual Strivings." In *A Native Son's Reader,* edited by Edward Margolies, pp. 12-19. Philadelphia: Lippincott, 1970.

_____. 1903b. "The Talented Tenth." In *The Black American,* edited by Leslie H. Fishel and Benjamin Quarles, pp. 226-228. Glenview, Ill.: Scott Foresman.

Jerome, Judson. 1971. *Culture out of Anarchy.* New York: Herder and Herder.

Mead, George Herbert. 1934. *Mind, Self and Society.* Edited by Charles W. Morris. Chicago; University of Chicago Press.

Morehouse College Bulletin. 1980. Winter.

Schumacher, E.F. 1973. *Small Is Beautiful.* New York: Harper & Row, Perennial Library.

U.S., Bureau of the Census. 1978. *Statistical Abstract of the United States: 1978*. Washington, D.C.: U.S. Government Printing Office.

Washington, Booker T. 1903. "Industrial Education for the Negro." In *The Black American,* edited by Leslie H. Fishel and Benjamin Quarles, pp. 223-228. Glenview, Ill: Scott Foresman.

Williams, Greer. 1959. *Virus Hunters.* New York: Knopf.

Willie, Charles V., and MacLeish, Marlene Y. 1976. "Priorities of Black College Presidents." *Educational Record* 57 (Spring):92-100.

2 Desegregation as a Way of Life: Living In, Between, and Beyond the Races

History is full of examples of creative marginality, of people who have lived not only in but also between and beyond the races of humankind. When separateness is being endorsed by blacks as well as by whites, and when integration as a national goal is under severe attack by liberals as well as by conservatives, there is a need to interpret these actions. This chapter is one such attempt.

The High Price of Tribalism

Given the present circumstances of American society and the racial tribal groups in which it is organized, integration in the near future does not seem to be an expected alternative. But neither is separatism a viable long-range option. This chapter describes the marginal people who live in, between, and beyond the races. It is they who are most likely to help our pluralistic society survive. The marginal people unite the clans and races in society and help us reconcile our differences.

We are ignoring the warnings of the past in our deliberate attempts to tribalize this nation and to frustrate the development of a genuine pluralistic community of interdependent people. When this nation was founded toward the close of the eighteenth century, its Constitutional Convention sanctioned slavery and racial discrimination. The first time this nation failed in human relationships, then, was at its beginning. It paid dearly for this failure after the middle of the nineteenth century with more than half a million lives lost in a civil war fought to end slavery, which could have been ended when the nation began.

Our nation did not learn from this tragic experience. At the close of the nineteenth century, the U.S. Supreme Court sanctioned racial segregation in its "separate but equal" doctrine. Again, we paid dearly for this miscarriage of justice. After the middle of the twentieth century, our urban communities began to go up in smoke as a kind of civil war returned to the streets of our cities. The number of dead has been mounting ever since.

From Charles V. Willie, *Oreo—On Race and Marginal Men and Women* (Wakefield, MA: Parameter Press, 1975), chap. 2. Used by permission of and special arrangement with the publishers of Parameter Press, Inc., Wakefield, Massachusetts. Copyright ©1975.

James B. Conant, former president of Harvard, became the chief prophet for public education in the late 1950s and early 1960s. In his famous book *Slums and Suburbs* (1961), Conant said that if integration in schools had occurred one hundred years ago when blacks were first made free, a different situation would exist today. He said a caste system finds its clearest manifestation in an educational system.

On the basis of my research (Willie and Levy 1972) concerning black students at white colleges and their high school experiences following the Supreme Court decision in 1954 (which outlawed racial segregation in public education), I conclude that life is different for those who experience racial integration. Youth who experience integrated education are likely to have more interracial contacts in college than college students who were not educated in integrated high schools.

Racial reconciliation occurs among people who meet one another. Racial reconciliation is not so much an attitude as it is an action. Conant suggested that the state of race relations in this country might be different today if black and white children had been educated together in the past. One black student at a predominantly white college analyzed his experience in this way: "If you don't try to bridge the gap, you just add to the troubles you already have—like prejudice, hate, and war." This young man's words were his own, but the wisdom they convey belongs to the ages.

In ancient times, Moses was a marginal man: born as a Hebrew slave, reared as a wealthy Egyptian, and eventually married to an Ethiopian or black woman ([Num. 12:1-3] the Cushites were from the land of Cush, identified as Ethiopia). In modern times, Martin Buber and Martin Luther King, Jr. lived in, between, and beyond their races. They too tried to reconcile the peoples of this world and left a legacy of creative marginality.

If marginality is so creative, why do so few aspire to be marginal people? Why are race and clan relationships exalted?

My hypothesis is that many people are fearful of marginality—are reluctant to live in, between, and beyond their race—because of their fear of loss of identity. They think they are maximizing their identity by relating primarily to like-minded and look-alike people when, in essence, they are limiting the range of their identity. Thus, they can be looked upon as suffering a partial loss of identity.

John Gardner (1968, pp. 145-146) describes identity as the assurance that comes from knowing and being known, and he calls the loss of identity a failure in the relationship between the individual and society. Gardner further states (1968 p. 148), "Those who suffer from a sense of anonymity [a loss of identity] would feel better if they could believe that their society needed them."

Identified by the Others

The search for identity thus seems to be a search for security and acceptance and a need to be needed by others. In the end, therefore, full identity depends upon one's actions as well as societal reactions, including the reactions of friends and enemies. Identity is a result of affirmation and confirmation, knowing and being known, needing and being needed. Identity involves personal action and group reaction.

This idea, of course, is different from the idea that identity can be found within oneself by drawing apart from the whole, by pulling apart from society at large. Identity, then, is a social process in which there is a negotiation between what a person thinks himself to be and what others believe him to be. The negotiating process is continuous, sometimes painful, sometimes pleasant. The anonymous people of this world, often referred to as invisible, are those who withdraw or who are pushed out of the social negotiating process. They suffer a loss of identity, either because they no longer affirm their personal significance or because others refuse to recognize and confirm their social worth.

The lives of the two Martins—Martin Buber and Martin Luther King, Jr.—are adequate examples of how one finds a wide-ranging identity and a sense of community by turning toward rather than away from the opposition and insisting on being recognized.

Martin Buber, for example, was a Zionist. Arthur Cohen (1957, p. 29) states that Zionism for many Jews became "the cloak of pride, the instrument of masking their alienation and lack of roots in European soil." For Buber, however, Zionism was "the means of renewing roots, the ultimate device of reestablishing, not surrendering, contact with the European tradition."

Beyond his connection with Europe, in 1938, when he was forced to leave Germany and go to Israel, Buber insisted that Israel ought to be a state of two nations in which Arabs and Jews should jointly participate and share. At one time he lived in the Arab sector of Israel. Moreover, he returned to Germany, amid much criticism, to receive the Peace Prize of the German Book Trade (Cohen 1957, p. 35).

Martin Luther King, Jr. was one of the greatest leaders this nation has ever experienced. His goal was total liberation for all people although his actual work was with poor black people. He always tried to achieve a double victory—one for the former oppressed and one for the former oppressors.

King saw the strength of black people as uniquely American. Yet he believed that there were similarities between the black struggle and the struggle of the people of Israel against the oppression of the ancient pharoah (1967, p. 170). He believed that black people ought to unite. Yet he said (1967, p. 150):

The future of the deep structural changes we seek will not be found in the decaying political machines. It lies in new alliances of Negroes, Puerto Ricans, labor, liberals, certain church and middle-class elements. (Copyright © 1967 by Martin Luther King, Jr. Reprinted by permission of Harper & Row.)

King was unhappy with the black power slogan because he believed it divided society and, to him, meant black domination rather than black equality. Yet he engaged in direct action in the public square as a powerful way of staging the case of blacks. He understood the origin of the black power slogan and presented the most incisive analysis of it that I have seen. His analysis is relevant to the discussion about identity (1967, pp. 32-33):

First, it is necessary to understand that Black Power is a cry of disappointment. The Black Power slogan did not spring full grown from the head of some philosophical Zeus. It was born from the wounds of despair and disappointment. It is a cry of daily hurt and persistent pain. For centuries the Negro has been caught in the tentacles of white power. Many Negroes have given up faith in the white majority because "white power" with total control has left them empty-handed. So in reality the call for Black Power is a reaction to the failure of white power. (Copyright © 1967 by Martin Luther King, Jr. reprinted by permission of Harper & Row.)

He further stated (1967, p. 40), "Anyone familiar with the Black Power movement recognizes that defiance of white authority and white power is a constant theme; the defiance almost becomes a kind of taunt." (Copyright © 1967 by Martin Luther King, Jr. Reprinted by permission of Harper & Row.)

Thus, the call for black power, according to the King analysis, is but another example of a failure in the relationship between the black individual and white society. Society has failed to make it clear that it needs black people. Accordingly, black people have begun to assert themselves in desperation to obtain the attention they need for survival. Riots are an irrational way of raging at a society that has neglected the oppressed.

Were there no challenges to the personal significance or the social survival of black people by white people, there would be no need to call for black power, no need to riot and rage.

The More a Group Is Threatened, the More It Unites

When group survival is threatened, then group identity is emphasized. Robert Park recognized this fact in his introduction to Everett Stonequist's *The Marginal Man.* Park (Stonequist 1937, p. xiii) said, "The loyalties that bind together the members of . . .the clan and the tribe . . . are in direct proportion to the intensity of the fears and hatreds with which they view their enemies and rivals in the larger intertribal . . . world." No group, black or white, can confirm its own identity. A group, like a person, may engage in self-affirmation but must be confirmed by another.

Speaking of individuals, Martin Buber said that the "essence of man . . . can be directly known only in a living relationship. Or the *I* . . . exists only through the relationship to the *Thou*" (1957, p. 205). Applying this principle to the races, one might assert that *blacks exist and are significant as a people, in part, through their relationship with whites; conversely, whites exist and are significant as a people, in part, through their relationship with blacks.*

When blacks or whites attempt to find meaning, security, and significance (which may be translated as identity) within themselves, they usually attempt this because the total society is not giving them these feelings. Other groups are not confirming the identity of the group that is trying to confirm its own identity. Self-confirmation, like self-love, is an action of doubtful value, arising from desperation. A group never can be really certain of its social significance in the scheme of things if only the members of that group believe it is valuable. A group rejected, ignored, or unrecognized tends to be uncertain of itself.

The two-stage process of identity—affirmation and confirmation—is necessary at all levels of society. It is necessary in the family and kinship or clan structure. Most people, black and white, are confirmed in their personhood in these structures. It is also necessary in the society at large.

The peoplehood status of whites tends to be confirmed by the society at large. The way of life of blacks, their various organizations and associations, are often ignored. Confirmation for personhood status at the family, kinship, or clan level is no substitute for confirmation of peoplehood status by the society at large.

James Coleman indicated how integrated education contributes to this confirmation at the society level: "Negro children in an integrated school come to gain a greater sense of their efficacy to control their destiny. It is very likely due to the fact that they see that they can do some things better than whites and can perform in school better than some whites, a knowledge which they never had so long as they were isolated in an all-black school" (1968, p. 25).

Melvin Tumin (1969, pp. 20-21) has said that the chances for acceptance are much greater when the outsiders have achieved powerful and prestigious social and economic positions. This is what is meant by the statement that "green money turns black people white." This, of course, is the error in most analyses of racial identity. They are based on a simplistic black-and-white analysis that assumes that all identity problems would be resolved if blacks would learn to think and act like whites. It is interesting to note that the statement is seldom reversed. It would appear to be unthinkable to say that whites could solve their identity problem by attempting to think and act like blacks. Yet this too must be considered as a possibility.

Confirming Our Value as Persons

Whites need confirmation of their personhood, just as do blacks. Almost automatically blacks have, in the past, confirmed the personhood of the whites. Blacks have always given confirmation, sometimes willingly sometimes grudgingly. Even when blacks speak disparagingly of a white, they may call him "the man"—a term that denotes humanity. But whites, speaking disparagingly of blacks, refer to them as "coons," "jungle bunnies," and other nonhuman animals. Whites have not so willingly confirmed the personhood of blacks. In fact, whites have been advised to practice "benign neglect" with reference to blacks. Hence, the preoccupation of blacks with their identity.

Indeed, one might conjecture that the separatist movement among blacks as manifested in the convening of a black caucus is threatening to some whites because it is a sign that blacks may take the next step and withhold or deny personhood confirmation for whites as whites did in their segregated groups in earlier years. Many whites, however, endorse the black separatist movement because of their misunderstanding of their need for blacks. As stated previously, because blacks have always confirmed the personhood of whites, many whites have never raised the question of what would happen to them if they were neglected by blacks. It is beyond the comprehension of many whites that they could be rejected by blacks, with harmful consequences.

The New Concept of the Marginal Person

An earlier concept of the marginal person was that of one who falls between two social or cultural groups (Stonequist 1937, p. 2). The new concept of the marginal person, as I see it, is of one who rises above two social or cultural groups, freeing the different groups to work together. Martin Buber and Martin Luther King, Jr. were the latter kind of marginal men. Of Martin Luther King, Jr. writer William Robert Miller (1968, p. 292) said, "In the end he was misunderstood . . . by both white liberals and black militants." At the time of King's death, Stokely Carmichael, the modern reviver of the idea of black power who challenged the leadership of King during the Mississippi March, said (quoted in Miller 1968, p. 292):

> When white America killed Dr. King . . . she lost it . . . He was the one man in our race who was trying to teach our people to have love, compassion and mercy for white people.

Also, it must be said that King was trying to teach white people to have love, compassion, and mercy for black people. Thus, he is the new marginal man who found his identity neither among blacks nor among whites but in the synthesis of these two races. Park conceived of the marginal person as one whom fate had condemned to live in two worlds. The new concept of the marginal person is one to whom fate has given the opportunity to unite two different worlds because one lives in, between, and beyond his or her social or cultural groups.

References

Buber, Martin. 1957. *Pointing the Way.* Edited and translated by Maruice S. Friedman. New York: Harper & Row Torchbooks.

Cohen, Arthur A. 1957. *Martin Buber.* New York: Hillary House.

Coleman, James. 1968. "Equality of Educational Opportunity." *Integrated Education* 6, no. 5 (September-October):19-28.

Conant, James B. 1961. *Slums and Suburbs.* New York: Macmillan.

Gardner, John W. 1968. *No Easy Victories.* New York: Harper & Row.

King, Martin Luther, Jr. 1967. *Where Do We Go from Here: Chaos or Community?* New York: Harper & Row (hardcover). Boston: Beacon Press (paperback).

Miller, William Robert. 1968. *Martin Luther King, Jr.: His Life, Martyrdom, and Meaning for the World.* New York: Weybright and Talley.

Stonequist, Everett V. 1937. *The Marginal Man.* New York: Scribner's.

Tumin, Melvin. 1969. *Comparative Perspectives on Race Relations.* Boston: Little, Brown & Co.

Willie, Charles V., and Levy, Joan D. 1972. "Black Is Lonely." *Psychology Today* 5, no. 10 (March):50.

3 Whites as the Minority: A New Educational Goal

The dominant people of power, the white majority, have from the beginning of this nation identified education as a means of indoctrination, a way of putting into place "the furniture of the mind." The subdominant people of power, the black minority, have turned to education as a means of liberation. On these two functions of education—indoctrination and liberation—blacks and whites disagree. With reference to race relations and education, part of the tension associated with school desegregation that has been generated during the past quarter of a century may be attributed to the fact that the majority does not realize that the educational goal of the minority also should be adopted as a standard for the nation.

Liberation as a Goal of Education

Consider the fussing and fighting that have ensued over the years about forced praying in the schools. The attempt to legislate a regular period of prayer is nothing short of an attempt by the majority to indoctrinate children into the way of religion as part of their education. The morning pledge of allegiance to the flag is also a way for the majority to indoctrinate students into loyalty to the government. Education also should be for liberation so that people are free to turn to the religion of their choice and are free to love the government that protects and sustains them.

Where there is not freedom, there is not love. As Joseph Fletcher (1966) has stated, love is the boss principle of life. For this reason, liberation ought to be a goal of education. It is the minority in this nation that has kept alive liberation as a goal of education. The *Brown* decision of the U.S. Supreme Court was part of the effort of minorities to achieve this goal. Liberation has been on the agenda of blacks for more than a century in this country.

In 1787, the year of the Constitutional Convention and one decade after the Declaration of Independence had been issued, the record shows that a group of black parents in Massachusetts petitioned the legislature of the commonwealth to make some provision for the education of their children. They had been denied admission to the public schools because of their race. The reasoning in the petition is of interest. The petitioners said that they were making this request so that their children would not grow up "in ignorance in a land of gospel light." Further, they said that education is a right that all free persons ought to enjoy (Kluger 1977, p. xi).

Shortly after emancipation, the former slaves exhibited an insatiable desire for learning. Booker T. Washington said, "It was a whole race trying to go to school. Few were too young, and none too old, to make the attempt to learn. As fast as any kind of teacher could be secured, not only were day-schools filled, but night-schools as well" (quoted by DuBois 1969, pp. 641-642). The continuing belief by blacks in the efficacy of education is illustrated by Bernice Stimley, a mother of four children all of whom graduated from college, three of whom received professional doctoral degrees from the Harvard Law School. On the occasion when she was honored in Chicago, Mrs. Stimley told Operation PUSH (People United to Save Humanity) and its president, the Reverend Jesse Jackson, that her philosophy of life was the same as that of her parents: You can have anything in life if you have an education (*Jet* 1978, p. 13).

James Comer, the famous black psychiatrist, said he went to school—"hurt feelings or no hurt feelings"—got an education, and got ahead. When his self-esteem was battered, his parents patched it up and sent him back into the battle. Eventually he became a member of the faculty of the Yale University Medical School and the author of several important books. Even though we know that adversity in getting an education can turn one off, Dr. Comer's experience has demonstrated that adversity also can turn one on (Comer 1972, p. 23). For Comer education was a means of liberation.

The point I am making is this. Integration was not the reason that the school cases were brought before the U.S. Supreme Court; it was liberation that the plaintiffs were seeking. For example, in the 1940s, the South Carolina state president of the National Association for the Advancement of Colored People (NAACP) told a Clarendon County church meeting that "the surest measure of the force with which the white man's heels was still pressing the black man's face into the mud was the schools." Then he asserted that the black schools of South Carolina were at that time a disgrace and concluded that "colored people could not rise until they got educated" (Kluger 1977, p. 13).

Historical Background

I do not intend to suggest that blacks invented the idea of education as a means of liberation for life and participation in a democracy. Actually, the idea set forth by black parents in Massachusetts in 1787 was similar to the one later articulated by Thomas Jefferson in 1813 about educating the masses to manage the concerns of society. Thomas Jefferson believed that the business of the state was to "establish the law for educating the common people." This should be accomplished through what he called "a general plan'' (National Park Service 1973). He said that education should provide the masses with "virtue and wisdom enough to manage the concerns of the society" (Jefferson 1813, p. 116).

According to Jefferson's general plan, every county would be divided into wards of five or six square miles. A free school supported by public resources would be established in each ward. The best students in the ward schools would be selected annually to study for higher degrees in free district schools. The most promising students in the district schools would be selected for education in a university that also would be publicly supported (Jefferson 1813, p. 116-118). In the South and elsewhere, there was opposition to Jefferson's ideas, particularly to those ideas pertaining to free public elementary and secondary schools for all. Free public education was not instituted in Virginia during Jefferson's lifetime.

In the South, during the early 1800s, "there was no general public educational system, . . . except perhaps, in North Carolina." According to W.E.B. DuBois, education was regarded by lower-class whites then "as a luxury connected with wealth." In Jefferson's Virginia, "less than one-half of the poor white children were attending any schools" (DuBois 1935, pp. 638-639). Slaves could receive no education; "the laws on this point were explicit and severe" (DuBois 1935, p. 638).

DuBois reported that the public school systems in most southern states began with the enfranchisement of the Negro (DuBois 1935, p. 648-649). The idea that the masses should be educated to participate effectively in the social order was implemented in the South during the Reconstruction period. All Americans, white as well as black in the South, owe a debt of gratitude to the state Reconstruction governments (some of which were dominated by blacks) for implementing the Jeffersonian idea of free public schools for all. A historian identified as Williams who was quoted by DuBois in his study of Reconstruction called the South Carolina public law that authorized tax-supported schools open to all "the most beneficial legislation the State . . . ever enacted" (quoted by DuBois 1935, p. 650). In 1868, black legislators initiated and supported the resolutions that eventually resulted in the formation of a South Carolina State Board of Education to oversee the development of free local public school systems in 1870. It was a case of the former oppressed accomplishing for their children and the children of their former oppressors what slaveowners like Thomas Jefferson could not accomplish.

Richard Korn, a scholar who has conducted extensive studies in criminology, commented upon this kind of outcome. He said, "This perhaps, is the . . . bigot's most bitter purgative: in the end he can be saved only by those who survived the worst he could do to them—his victims" (Korn 1968, p. 196).

In states such as South Carolina and Louisiana, the Reconstruction governments in which blacks played leading roles prohibited separation by race in their new public school systems (DuBois 1935, p. 663). Meanwhile, some influential white-dominated groups that had manifested considerable interest in the education of blacks continued to lobby for racial segregation. For example, at the national level, the trustees of the Peabody Fund were credited with causing the U.S. Congress to drop a clause in the original draft of the Civil Rights Act of 1875 that would have prohibited separate schools in this nation (DuBois 1935, p. 663).

This brief historical analysis has taught us what sociologist Robert Merton discovered a few years ago: "it is not infrequently the case that the non-conforming minority in a society represents the interests and ultimate values of the group more effectively than the conforming majority" (1968, p. 421). As we have seen, blacks intended that education as a means of liberation for participation in a democracy should be available to all.

School Desegregation Plans

Without recognizing the valuable contribution of blacks in the past toward public education for everyone in this nation, whites in general have assumed that desegregation basically is for the benefit of blacks. This assumption was the first and great error that misguided the implementation of most school desegregation plans. Based on his study, *Equality of Educational Opportunity,* James Coleman and associates concluded that "there is evidence in the short run, an effect of school integration on the reading and mathematics achievement of Negro pupils, [and that] in the long run, integration should be expected to have a positive effect on Negro achievement" (1966, p. 7). Thus, the push toward integrating blacks with whites in predominantly white schools was accelerated because of the expectation that the higher achievement level by whites would somehow improve black achievement.

The definition of education as achievement in cognitive areas is too narrow. Education as liberation has been forgotten in most school desegregation plans. The idea of education as liberation has been forgotten even by some advisers to the black plaintiffs in school desegregation cases. When Judge W. Arthur Garrity's final order for a school desegregation plan for Boston was issued, an officer of the Boston chapter of the NAACP said that the order, in general, was a good one, but that he would examine it carefully to determine whether it desegregated all schools. The NAACP officer said he would examine the order to determine "whether there are any schools left which are predominantly black." He implied that there should not be any such schools and stated that this was the requirement that must be met (Willie 1978, p. 15).

The point that was missed is that in any good school desegregation plan there ought to be some schools that are predominantly black or brown, so that whites can have the beneficial experience of learning as a minority.

In this nation, minorities have kept alive the concept of education as liberation. A liberating education focuses on truth as well as honesty, justice, and altruism. Whites need to learn these concepts as much as blacks need to learn language and mathematical skills. This fact seems to have been forgotten by some black as well as white advocates of school desegregation.

When the Boston news media were taking stock of the second year of court-ordered school desegregation, the education editor of the *Boston Globe* began an article assessing the experience: "The Boston schools are on their way up. Slowly. Reading scores are holding the rise of last year." The article continued: "Preliminary reading tests results . . . show . . . gains for minority children but no loss for whites." In other words, school desegregation had benefited blacks and had not harmed whites. There was no discussion of whether Boston school children had gained more knowledge of the functions of the court in a democratic society or had developed a better understanding of justice, equality, and equity as a result of school desegregation. The knowledge of these concepts has to do with liberation. Bostonians were more interested in whether school desegregation was enabling blacks to conform more closely to the achievement levels of whites (Willie 1978, p. 80).

Despite their belief that desegregation basically was for the benefit of blacks, whites have profited from school desegregation because of their association with blacks. In South Boston, a predominantly working-class white homogeneous area where school desegregation was resisted, a school official indicated a positive outcome for whites. The blacks who came to South Boston High School inspired more whites to go to college. According to this school official, "The 'in' thing with blacks is going to college and that was a boon to Southie where almost no one goes [to college]. . . . The very feeling [blacks] had about going to college had a good effect on the white kids . . . the white kids have downgraded themselves, felt college was too tough or that they didn't have the ability . . . now there is a feeling [among whites] that 'if blacks are going [to college], why can't we?' . . . It's rubbed off on the white kids [of South Boston]." Nowhere in any of the analytical discussions of desegregation by social scientists and educational researchers is there acknowledgement of what whites have learned from blacks as a result of school desegregation (Willie 1978, pp. 80-81). Thus, in the 1970s and 1980s we have continued a practice that began in the 1870s and 1880s of failing to recognize how blacks have benefited whites in terms of education.

Benefits of Minority Status

There is evidence that the quality of education for blacks in terms of the acquisition of communication and calculation skills has improved, and this improvment is associated with desegregation. The failures of school desegregation to date, then, are related to what it has not done for whites. It has not provided ample opportunity for whites to enjoy the benefits of minority status. What one learns as a minority is different from what one learns as a member of the majority.

Let me share with you what minority status did for Benjamin Mays, a distinguished black educator, who attended predominantly white Bates College in Maine in 1917:

> One of my dreams came true at Bates. Through competitive experience, I had finally dismissed from my mind for all time the myth of the inherent inferiority of all Negroes and the inherent superiority of all whites—articles of faith to so many in my previous environment. I had done better in academic performance, in public speaking, and in argumentation and debate than the vast majority of my classmates. I conceded academic superiority to not more than four in my class. I had displayed more initiative as a student leader than the majority of my classmates. Bates College made these things possible. Bates College did not "emancipate" me; it did the far greater service of making it possible for me to emancipate myself, to accept with dignity my own worth as a free man. Small wonder that I love Bates College! (Mays 1971, p. 60).

Few desegregation plans have reassigned substantial numbers of whites to schools in which they would be a minority. By not experiencing minority status whites have not had the opportunity to erase from their minds for all times the myth of the inherent superiority of all whites, articles of faith that still persist in white-dominated schools, agencies, and other institutions. School desegregation can emancipate whites from a sense of superiority if whites are provided the opportunity of serving as a minority. A most valuable experience that many whites have missed is that of being a minority.

One reason why we have not understood the debilitating learning effects of perpetual majority status upon whites is that we have relied too heavily as educator upon the U.S. Supreme Court decision, which was a legal document, and have not appropriately supplemented it with the finding from social science regarding the consequences of segregation. The Supreme Court opinion stated that "to separate [children in grade and high school] from others of similar age and qualifications solely because of their race generates a feeling of inferiority [in the children of the minority group] as to their status in the community that may effect their hearts and minds in a way unlikely ever to be undone" (*Brown* v. *Board of Education* 1954).

The Court was silent about what segregation does to the children of the majority group because they were not plaintiffs in the court cases. I contend that segregation has generated a feeling of superiority in the children of the majority group as to their status in the community and has affected their hearts and minds in a way unlikely ever to be undone unless they are exposed to the experience of being a minority.

By remaining silent about what segregation has done to the white majority, the Supreme Court contributed to the educational myth that desegregation essentially was for the benefit of blacks and not whites. In the *Brown II* decision (1955) the U.S. Supreme Court gave district courts the privilege of "tak[ing] into account the public interest in the elimination of such obstacles [in the administration of public schools . . . on a non-discriminatory basis]." If whites assumed that they were superior to blacks and school desegregation was for the purpose of overcoming "a feeling of inferiority [in the children of the minority group]," as declared by the Supreme Court, then the public interest would appear to be best served by integrating black and brown children into predominantly white schools. This is precisely what was done. The court did not recognize the sense of superiority on the part of white children as a defect in their education. But I recognize it as a defect.

A statement by a Richmond, Virginia school official is an example of this sense of superiority on the part of whites. He said to me that "the white middle-class American will not submerge his values to those of an antithetical culture" and that "white middle-class America will accept a 15 to 20 percent black population in his child's school if they are middle class." Thus, in the Richmond school desegregation case the school board proposed that two counties that were adjacent to the city should be consolidated with the Richmond school district. The Richmond school system was 80 to 85 percent black. If the suburban areas had been added, the consolidated school district would have been 70 percent white. Such an arrangement would have protected against submerging the values of white middle-class Americans to those of blacks and, in the opinion of the school board, would have been in the public interest. The arrangement was disallowed.

A similar arrangement was proposed with reference to local government in Jacksonville, Florida several years ago. That arrangement prevailed. Under the slogan of good government, whites launched a movement to consolidate city and county governments, as the numbers of whites declined. The surrounding Duval County was populated predominantly with whites; they controlled the county but wanted to retain city power too. They launched a consolidation campaign and won (Willie 1977, p. 1949). By winning, whites lost the opportunity to be a minority in schools and other local institutions in that setting.

My message, then, is simple. Desegregation should move ahead with more than deliberate speed and should guarantee the continuation of predominantly black and brown schools so that whites can have the benefit of being a minority. It is time that we declare that predominantly black and brown institutions also are in the public interest.

We know that most whites who attend predominantly black schools lose a sense of superiority, just as many blacks (such as Benjamin Mays) who attend predominantly white schools get rid of feelings of inferiority. In 1978 the Southern Regional Education Board published a study conducted by Nancy Standley of white students at black public colleges and universities which found that the idea most strongly internalized by a large majority of whites in predominantly black schools was that "a student's race does not affect his or her ability to learn" (Standley 1978, pp. 36-39). In other words, white students had to go to a black school to discover that they were not always superior. Such learning is of value and should be spread and increased among whites. Findings from the Standley study will be analyzed in greater detail in chapter 9.

If through true education there is liberation (and the record of blacks in humanizing this nation attests to this fact), then the next twenty-five years should be devoted to delivering a liberating education to a significant number of whites who can make a difference.

Implementation of Liberation

We must remember, however, that blacks cannot liberate whites. Whites must liberate themselves even as blacks had to liberate themselves. It was not until blacks decided to cease cooperating in their own oppression that they got off the back of the bus and sat down at the lunch counter. Blacks ceased cooperating in their own oppression when they indicated with their bodies on the line that they were willing to make the sacrifices and suffer the consequences of leading a liberated life. There are some whites who are now ready to be liberated and to be liberators. But they need black schooling.

My favorite philosopher, Martin Buber, has stated that the liberator is not a slave but is connected with the slaves and usually is socialized in the alien community so that he or she knows all that one needs to know to transcend existing custom and convention (1946, p. 35). History has demonstrated the truth of this principle. As mentioned in chapter 2, Moses liberated the ancient people of Israel and led them from Egyptian captivity, was Hebrew by birth and nature but was reared in the household of the Pharaoh as his daughter's adopted son. Moses understood Hebrew society because his mother was his nursemaid, but he also knew the Egyptian society and its secrets, and thus he was able to overcome. Gandhi, who gave leadership to the movement to overcome the British colonial captivity of

India, led an ascetic life as if he were an Indian peasant. But Gandhi was a London-trained lawyer. He knew and understood both India and England and, therefore, was able to liberate India. Then there was Martin Luther King, Jr. who came here, blessed our souls, and went away. To blacks and others in America, he was a liberator, saint, and spiritual leader. He understood black culture but also knew white customs. He was a More-house College graduate and more. During his formative years, he studied in a predominantly white seminary in Chester, Pennsylvania and in a predominantly white university in Boston, Massachusetts. Martin Buber was right: the liberator is conected to the culture of the people to be freed, but is not dominated by their customs, and is knowledgeable of the way of life of others.

There are some whites who are now ready to liberate themselves and their population from the oppressive and enslaving ideology of white supremacy. This is another way of saying that there are whites connected to the culture of whites who are now ready to learn from blacks in order to liberate themselves. However, they do not have full opportunities to learn. Contacts with blacks are too limited.

Blacks do not have the right to hoard the liberating methods that they have developed through years of suffering. If whites are to overcome their debilitating belief in white superiority, they must be tutored through pro-longed association with blacks who can serve as mentors during their for-mative years. Whites must be taught the meaning of suffering, sacrifice, and service as only blacks can teach them. Whites must be taught about honesty, justice, and altruism and learn how to be merciful, forgiving, and trusting. Whites can be taught these things by black and brown people who have been merciful, forgiving, and trusting. Whites can learn to overcome their enslavement to the false idea that they are supreme only if they have the privilege of living as a trusting minority. Predominantly black schools can provide this kind of liberating education for whites and, consequently, save our country from tribal warfare.

In 1969, the year after Martin Luther King, Jr. died, white foundations issued money to good white colleges in the North to recruit black students. These foundations said that they were trying to bring black students into the mainstream. There is more than one stream, however. We reject the conclu-sion that America is what whites are. Robert Merton was right. The non-conforming minority sometimes represents the basic values of the society better than the conforming majority.

There is a simple psychological principle that blacks must deal with: one can help people only with people. Thus, if whites are to be helped to overcome a sense of white supremacy, blacks must help them; likewise, blacks who were helped to overcome a sense of inferiority were aided by whites.

As a beginning goal, all black schools, including public and private black colleges, should recruit 20 percent of their student body from whites who are ready to be redeemed from the ideology of racial supremacy. There are approximately forty-five thousand students enrolled in private black colleges. The great foundations of this country should be petitioned through the United Negro College Fund or some other organization to support with scholarship assistance ten thousand white students at the private predominantly black college campuses so that they may be helped with a new kind of education that emphasizes justice and liberation. Already the white enrollment at public predominantly black colleges is 15 percent. Scholarship money is necessary to recruit some white students. All whites are not affluent. Some rural and inner-city whites are poor. Black schools can help redeem such whites from poverty, and these whites in turn might help redeem the nation from snobbery.

References

Brown v. *Board of Education of Topeka.* 1954. 347 U.S. 483.

Brown II. 1955. 349 U.S. 294.

Buber, Martin. 1946. *Moses.* Reissue. New York: Harper, 1958.

Coleman, James S., Campbell, Ernest Q., Hobson, Carol J., McPartland, James, Mood, Alexander, Wienfield, Frederic, York, R. 1966. *Equality of Educational Opportunity.* Washington, D.C.: U.S. Government Printing Office.

Comer, James. 1972. *Beyond Black and White.* New York: Quadrangle Books.

DuBois, W.E.B. 1935. *Black Reconstruction in America in 1860-1880.* Reissue. New York: Atheneum, 1969.

Fletcher, Joseph. 1966. *Situation Ethics.* Philadelphia: Westminster Press.

Jefferson, Thomas. 1813. "Letters from Thomas Jefferson to John Adams on Natural Aristocracy." In *We Hold These Truths*, edited by Stuart Gary Brown. New York: Harper, 1941.

Jet Magazine. 27 July 1978, p. 13.

Kluger, Richard. 1975. *Simple Justice.* New York: Vintage Books.

Korn, Richard R. 1968. *Juvenile Delinquency.* New York: Crowell.

Mays, Benjamin E. 1971. *Born to Rebel.* New York: Scribner's.

Merton, Robert K. 1968. *Social Theory and Social Structure.* New York: Free Press.

National Park Service. 1973. *Thomas Jefferson Memorial Pamphlet.* Washington, D.C.: U.S. Government Printing Office.

Standley, Nancy V. 1978. *White Students Enrolled in Black Colleges and Universities.* Atlanta: Southern Regional Education Board.

Willie, Charles V. 1977. *Black/Brown/White Relations.* New Brunswick, N.J.: Transaction Books.

―――― . 1978. *The Sociology of Urban Education.* Lexington, Mass.: Lexington Books.

Part II
Recruitment, Admissions, and Retention

4

Recruitment and Financial Aid

At four predominantly white, public and private, two-year and four-year institutions that I studied in New York State, the enrollment of black students was less than 2 percent. The schools were making a major effort to increase the number of blacks on campus, but most for various reasons had not made much progress.

Recruitment of Black Students by Other Students

A method of recruiting black students that appeared to be successful in some of the schools was the involvement of black students in the recruitment of other blacks. Gretchen, a freshman at Metropolitan College, is a member of a group of black students who go to local high schools to talk with black graduating seniors about continuing their education. In these recruitment missions, specific information about the college faculty, scholarships, and other kinds of aid is shared. Also, high school students are told about the black organizations on campus. The Union of Black Collegians and the student Afro-American Society have been particularly helpful in recruiting black students. Several students in these organizations have been asked to take on recruitment assignments in their hometowns. One student was especially pleased that her college had encouraged the black organizations to recruit "hard-core ghetto students" for the next semester. As stated by Glenn, a student, "We recruit a lot of people. We're trying to recruit more kids. Whenever we go to a party or any place, we talk about this college. We hope to get 100 kids here next year." Presently, there are fewer than forty black students on his college campus.

The black students are not pleased with the current number of blacks on any of the campuses included in our study. They believe that there should be more. They place the major responsibility for recruitment upon the administrative personnel, although they are willing to participate in the recruitment process. The administration at most white colleges is accused by some blacks of not being sufficiently aggressive in the recruitment of black students.

Reprinted with permission from *Black Students at White Colleges*, by Charles V. Willie and Arline McCord (New York: Praeger Publishers, 1972), chap. 7. This chapter has been slightly revised.

Even though they cooperate by participating in recruitment programs, many black students continue to be deeply suspicious of the motives and intentions of the administrators and are quick to charge admissions officers with bad faith. Tom said, "We go home to our high schools and tell them about Small City College and tell them to write. They have, but they haven't gotten an answer. I guess the administration can tell by where they live that they are blacks." A middle-aged graduate student, Rosie Mae, enrolled in a small department in Cosmopolitan College, has been asked to be in charge of the recruitment committee of her department. She believes that she has been asked to assume this responsibility because she is the only black student in that department. Even though she has accepted this responsibility, she said, "I . . . feel that recruitment should be a paid position that Cosmopolitan College should be in charge of." There is a hint in Rosie Mae's remarks that she believes that she is being exploited. Yet she and others who grumble from time to time are willing to participate in recruitment because it offers the possibility of enlarging the black student population on campus. Thus, the recruitment of black students is a project in which the administration and blacks cooperate, despite the one-sided or mutual suspicion that may exist. From a black perspective, more blacks on campus means political power and an enriched social and educational life.

Black Students' Perspective on Recruitment

Black students believe that the college will use the enlarged black population on campus as evidence to refute allegations of racism that have been lodged against many white institutions. Black students believe that the white colleges they attend are more interested in keeping their own images clean than in providing a relevant education for blacks. The black students also believe that the public institutions are recruiting them mainly because they are required to participate in specially funded programs for minority students. The blacks insist that the colleges should do more than recruit only a token number of racial minorities.

Indeed, the awkward way in which some of the schools have gone about recruiting blacks when no black staff members were available to help has contributed to the impressions mentioned. These are the remarks of several black students in a rap session at Little Village College:

Do you think the administration is hesitant to bring more blacks on campus?

I think they have within the administration some kind of quota, you know, an amount they gotta drag in—one hundred or two hundred blacks.

They realize now that they have to have so many black students on their campus. In other words we're token niggers on the campus.

This is really the reason they get black men on campus: 'Cause they have to have them.

What about the people that come? I mean, what type of person recruits the black people?

Well, Mr. Green. Now they appointed him as a recruiter for black students because he headed a black regiment while serving in the war. So they figure: "Well, he's had a little to do with black people, so maybe he'd be the best since he went through this." This might sound funny but it's true.

Did you talk with Mr. Green before you came here?

Right! I did. Mr. Green came to my high school. They came in the winter. They were pretty friendly. But the way he put it—like he needed us for some reason beside education, you know. He was too quick—like: "You can come. I'll live with you, too," you know.

Did he say that?

Not in the same words. That's what the overall picture was.

I got the same impression, man. I talked with him over the phone. . . . My cousin goes here; he's a senior. He said, "Call Mr. Green, man." I called him and said, "Mr. Green, I'm interested in your college and from what my cousin told me, it sounds like a pretty good deal. So I would like very much to apply there and see if I could get in." He said, "Don't worry about that. You're in. You're automatically in."

I went to see this guy that was the recruiter for two-year colleges. And he told me to get my application and everything and send them to Little Village College. Now, this was the end of July, almost the beginning of August. And the second or third week in August, I was accepted.

Did they know you were black?

Hell, yeah!

On the Education Opportunity Grant program?

You bet your life!

That's a shame, man. It's not a shame. But, you know, just the system they got up here. . . .

That's the one generalization I get about Little Village College. . . . They'll accept us just as long as we're black. No matter how we're qualified. You know what I mean? They'll put us in a program; they'll put us in a major, and knowing we can't make it, but just putting us there because we're black.

Knowing we can't make it!

So much money was appropriated last year for black students and because
Little Village College has so few. . . . So they had to accept so many but
not over a certain amount for this school.

From the foregoing, it is clear that the relationship between black
students and white colleges is characterized by deep-seated distrust by
blacks, even when financial opportunities are provided by the schools.
Because of this persisting feeling, it is most important that white colleges
involve black staff in the recruitment and admissions process. Black
students tend to believe that there is a greater chance that black staff will
be more interested in the welfare of the individual than in the image of the
institution.

Despite the awkwardness of recruiting officers, the previous remarks of
the students demonstrate that visiting and talking directly with black
students is a successful method of recruitment. Several students indicated
that they came to a particular college because a representative personally
approached them at their high schools or elsewhere in their hometown communities.

The utilization of black students, then, is a very successful way of
recruiting other black students. Black students are willing to participate in
recruitment programs because of self-interest. This explains why some
black students will invite other blacks to become members of a white college
community that they admittedly distrust.

The high school counselor also may be of some significance in referring
black students to white colleges. Of the black students, 25 percent said that
a high school counselor suggested a particular institution—in many instances, the counselor contacted the admissions office on behalf of the student and worked out special support arrangements. Nevertheless, approximately 75 percent of the black students made their way to college without
the assistance of a counselor. The meaning of this fact is unclear, but it does
suggest that the influence of the counselor is not pervasive.

Financial Aid and Economic Resources

A college must offer liberal financial aid if it is to recruit minority students.
In this study of midwestern colleges, Warren W. Willingham (1970, p. 7)
discovered that 80 percent of the minority students needed financial aid. My
study indicates that limited income created similar problems for black
students in New York State. Black students in white colleges come, as a
rule, from families with modest economic resources. The median annual income for the fathers of black students is only two-thirds as large as the median yearly income for the fathers of white students.

I found that about 6 percent of the black students' families could be classified as extremely poor, and another 6 percent as very affluent. The picture among whites was different. At least 25 percent of the white students had families who were very affluent, and only 3 to 4 percent were extremely poor. Very affluent households had annual incomes that were more than twice as large as the median for the total population, and very poor households existed on incomes that were less than the upper limit of the official poverty range.

The income of many fathers, both white and black, is not sufficient for the skyrocketing costs of a college education. Dual employment of mother and father often is required. Women worked in a majority of both black and white households that had college students: 61 percent of the white mothers and 78 percent of the black mothers. Looked at in another way, one might say that the proportion of mothers not in the labor force in households with college-matriculating students is almost twice as great for white households (39 percent), as compared with black households (22 percent).

Because of their disadvantaged circumstances, most of the black students (nearly nine out of every ten) believed that scholarships especially designed for blacks should be set aside. Blacks contend that it creates false hope to open the doors of white colleges but not provide the necessary financial aid. On the other hand, a majority of white students (about seven out of every ten) believe that special scholarships should not be reserved exclusively for blacks. The white students did not volunteer any opinions on what adjustments they thought should be made to compensate for the unequal financial circumstances of black and of white families. The belief of some whites that blacks are receiving preferential treatment has been a bone of contention between black and white students.

The economic resources of many black parents are too limited to allow them to pay for a college education for their children while maintaining the regular expenses of a household. Of the black students enrolled in the four colleges in my New York State study, 63 percent were supported by sources other than their parents. Only 46 to 47 percent of the white students said they had to rely on nonfamily resources. A majority of the white college students (53.5 percent) received some support from their parents, but this was the experience of only 38 percent of the black students. Nearly two-thirds of the black students (63 percent) receive financial aid from their schools, including direct grants and compensation for work on campus. Approximately 22 percent of the black students received assistance from other sources not specified. When the black students who receive financial support from unspecified sources other than parents are added to those identified as receiving direct support from their schools, the proportion of assisted students is similar to the 80 percent of minority students who require financial aid reported in the study of midwestern colleges by Willingham.

The black students at the white colleges came from a wide variety of backgrounds. Among the occupations represented by their parents are farm laborers, construction workers, physicians, insurance agents, telephone operators, case workers, barbers, beauticians, private household workers, restaurant owners, public school teachers, nurses, bus drivers, and postal workers. The black population on these white college campuses is diversified. Black students have grown up in all sorts of family structures and living arrangements. They come mainly from working-class and lower middle-class families. Their general feeling of financial uncertainty derives from the modest family income and their dependency on nonfamily sources of support, which many black students describe as untrustworthy. This feeling of uncertainty was found again and again to serve as a distraction from their studies.

Although the proportion of black students (57 percent) who talk about their money worries with other students is not much different from the proportion of white students (51 percent) who often carry on conversations about this topic, our interviews revealed some special problems and frustrations for blacks. At private colleges, money problems for black students are particularly severe. Anne is a freshman student from a rural community. Her mother and father work in a foreign country. Her remarks are typical.

The one thing I really found disillusioning about Cosmopolitan College is the lack of financial output they have. When you are on the outside and not in close quarters with the college, you hear they have so much money. Guidance counselors tell you that Cosmopolitan College has a lot of money to give for financial aid. They don't give it to the black students. And most of the black students need it.

By the time I finish school, if I go at the rate I'm going, I'll have large loans on my back at the end of four years. I only have a partial scholarship from the college.

They charge late fees for everything. My tuition was late this time because my parents are out of the country. Where was I supposed to get it from? I don't know. The finances are just crippling. . . .

I started to work as soon as I got here at T____ and P____ as a telephone solicitor. I lasted a week and a half. I was working five nights a week, four hours a night, and I just couldn't take it. Then I worked at the campus store. That was all right but I still didn't like the idea of going to school and working too. I stopped working at the campus store at the beginning of this semester. All of my spending money is gone. I just can't afford to keep going. I don't know what is going to happen next year.

The way you hear about it, you think, "Oh great, I'll apply and get some financial aid." And then you don't get it. Every time you don't make the average grade . . . they take away a portion of your scholarship or something like that. . . . What's taking away scholarship money going to do? All it's going to do is keep you away from coming here next semester.

You already put so much out; it's a waste not to continue really. I'd like to get financial aid, I'd do all right if I had that.

Several students commented about the scaling down of financial aid during subsequent years of matriculation. "If a person was needy when he got here, he should be much more needy after the tuition raise," said Charles, a third-year student. He reasoned that one's scholarship should go up instead of down. He stated that after the college enrolls a black student, financial aid is frequently cut, "which was, after all, one of the basic things that got me here in the first place." He asserted that his college is losing black students because of this practice. Cynthia, a student from a large family, also complained about the administration of financial aid at Cosmopolitan College. "The financial aid policy which makes it possible for the administration to take back a scholarship at their discretion creates hardships, especially for black students." She went on to say that "a large number of black students could not stay at Cosmopolitan College without financial aid; as a result, if they lose their scholarships they usually must leave school." Cynthia was particularly resentful of this financial relationship between black students and the college administration, which she characterized as "dependency" for blacks. A final observation comes from Arthur, a sophomore psychology major, whose father is a production helper in an upstate New York industrial community. Arthur believed that the financial aid office looks upon black students as potential financiers of their own education. "They don't seem to realize that black students have grave financial problems. We don't have mothers and fathers with high-paying jobs and sometimes there are a lot of children in the family." Most black students firmly believed that more blacks would go to college if there was more financial aid available.

At this point, it should be reiterated that our study is from the point of view of black students. The financial aid officers can field most of these complaints with perfectly reasonable answers from their point of view. The answers, however, may be inadequate from the point of view of black students. Insecurity and uncertainty have been their lot for so long that any attempt, legitimate or otherwise, to take away any benefits they have been given is immediately interpreted as a conspiracy to keep blacks down. Because of the racial inequality in family income, demonstrated in this and other studies, blacks are particularly edgy about financial manipulations. More than 70 percent of the blacks attending these colleges say that they are there because it is very important that they be able to look forward to a secure future. Approximately 40 percent of the black students (compared with 14 percent of the white students) say it is very important that their college education provide them with the opportunity to earn a great deal of money. It is fair to say that a majority of both white and black students hope that a college education will contribute to their personal growth and develop skills that will enable them to help others. However, the deprived circumstances of most blacks cause the economic opportunities that college may open up to be very significant to them. Any reduction in college financial aid, therefore, is a threat to the education and future security of young black people.

Blacks have historical evidence that whites are not likely to deal fairly with them in money matters. College blacks have the current reactions of their white classmates as evidence too. Daily, they are confronted with attitudes such as those revealed in this study.

Although 73 percent of the white students believed that the college should provide tutorial and other special help for black students having problems in school work, only 40 percent believed that financial aid, such as special scholarships, should be reserved for blacks. Perhaps most whites oppose special opportunities for blacks because they believe that there is no discrimination and, therefore, no need for preferential treatment. Indeed, 75 percent of the white students believed that there was equal access to scholarships and other financial aids at their schools.

The many complaints about financial aid indicate that some administrative officers at white colleges are insensitive to the severe economic deprivation of black people. These complaints also indicate that white colleges have not faced up to the financial dimensions of increasing the black student population.

On the basis of our analysis, it would appear that white colleges are interested in recruiting more black students and that blacks attending these schools have a similar interest. Black students tend to believe that they and the white colleges have different reasons for recruiting blacks, but, nevertheless, they are willing to cooperate because of the benefit they will derive from an enlarged black student body.

The coming together of black students and white college administrators around a common recruitment program, in which each is benefiting for different reasons, is significant. It indicates that self-interest is an important component of social action and that it is possible to unite disparate groups in a common cause if each group can fulfill its desires by completing the task jointly.

Reference

Willingham, Warren W. 1970. *Admission of Minority Students in Midwestern Colleges*. Evanston, Ill.: College Entrance Examination Board.

5 Standardized Testing for Admissions: A New Form of Status Politics

The movement in states throughout the United States to define and measure minimal competencies that students are expected to attain before leaving high school essentially is a political movement according to a report entitled *Private Premises and Public Purposes: A State Defines Minimal Competencies* (Daniels 1977). Daniels concluded that "the definition [of minimal competencies] has only limited utility." Nevertheless, "the [state] agency," he observed, "can use the definition politically . . . to show critics of the schools' performance that it is making a serious effort to improve productivity by setting standards in terms of specific learning outcomes" 1977, p. iii). Daniels indicated that these agencies may use such data not so much to help students as to defend themselves.

If the movement for minimal competence testing is indeed political, we should reflect upon the process of defining what is measured and why. Irving Horowitz (1972, p. 7) tells us that "the decision to conceptualize the developmental process, in terms of one model rather than the other, is often made on the basis of strategy rather than on the basis of scientific warrant." Horowitz was discussing the development of nations, but his wisdom also is applicable to the development of individuals. Thus, Horowitz alerts us to the fact that "moral assumptions and predilections necessarily enter into both conceptual categories and research operations" (Horowitz 1972, p. 3).

Minimal Competencies

In the light of these observations, the following questions must be entertained: "What exactly are minimal competencies—and who says so?" (Daniels 1977, p. i). The who-says-so question is crucial and must be answered first before determining what the competencies are.

Several years ago H.H. Remmers conducted a series of surveys among teenagers and discovered that the development of vocational skills and knowledge about our society were important to some of them. However, a higher proportion thought that "knowing how to get along with other people" was the most important thing that young people should get out of high school (Remmers and Radler 1962, p. 140). The skill of learning how to get along with others that was valued by approximately one out of every three

45

young people in the Remmers and Radler study probably differs from the skill or skills that adults would classify as most important to obtain from a high school education. What skills then should be included in a determination of minimal competencies—those skills valued highly by adults or those skills valued highly by youth?

The parents of many young people value the development of skills that will lead to a high-paying professional or managerial job as an outcome of formal education. In the television series about six American families, Stanley Pasciak—a blue-collar worker, the father in a Chicago Polish-American family—manifested this orientation. Of his son's attempt to break into drama and acting in California, he said: "You tell what you are doing. But then what your salary is, what your pay is, it doesn't seem to fit the title. I'm always going back to the financial end. . . . To me, success is when . . . the money rolls in. That's success, isn't it? I think it is. . . . You got to make a living" (Wilkes 1977, p. 32).

This orientation is not limited to working-class adults. When Judson Jerome, a college teacher, began his professional career, he almost felt compelled to explain the value of any course he taught in terms of a dollar sign (Jerome 1971). Surely these values of adults—middle-class as well as working-class—are not less significant than those of youth. Yet the values of youth also are important. Clearly, there is contradiction in what is valued by different sectors of the society. The questions posed earlier about the definition of minimal competencies and whose prerogative it is to define them acknowledge these differences.

Despite these contradictions, standardized testing has become a way of life in American society. Of the many standardized tests, those of aptitude, achievement, and competencies probably are more important because the score that one obtains on one of these tests often determines whether or not further educational opportunities will be denied or made available to an individual. A large number of colleges are members of the College Entrance Examination Board, "and practically all of them required their applicants to take at least the Scholastic Aptitude Test" (Angoff and Dyer 1971, p. 5).

Exclusion of Minorities

The regents of the University of California have approved an admissions policy that is described as "more stringent" because it "gives greater weight to the standardized test scores than to high school grade point averages." The policy was proposed by the university's faculty and commended by the university's president as a corrective to "a decline in the quality of preparation among incoming freshmen" (*New York Times,* 30 May 1977). By the university's own reckoning, "the new admissions policy would exclude less than 2 percent of white freshmen, 8.8 percent of black students and 9.5 percent of those called 'Latinos.' '' This projection of the effect of the new admissions policy that relies more on standardized test scores was based on a study of entering freshmen in 1976 before implementation of the policy (*New York Times,* 30 May 1977). One function of the standardized test, according to the results of the University of California's own study, is to disproportionately exclude minorities. Other experiences with standardized testing outside the academy have revealed similar function.

The exclusion of minorities and women has been the consequence of standardized tests administered to prospective government workers. The tests are given, presumably, to determine if the test takers are able to perform specific jobs. The Civil Service Commission of New Jersey was hauled into court by the State Public Advocates Office about these standardized tests. It had received a number of complaints "that tests bore little or no relationship to the jobs" (*New York Times,* 28 October 1977, B3). "The New Jersey Civil Service Commission acknowledged . . . that its testing system has been inadequate regarding women and minorities," and the chairman of the commission said that "it was possible that the tests being used might work against certain races because of the 'culture' of the persons who drafted the tests" (*New York Times,* 28 October 1977, B3).

The charge most frequently lodged against some standardized tests is that they are biased against racial minorities and the poor. Caroline Hodges Persell (1977, p. 63) stated that "Most . . . scholastic aptitude tests used in schools are nationally standardized on white middle-class populations." Another charge against some of these tests is that they determine how well one may perform the first year in school but not how well one may perform in a particular vocation over the years. A third charge against some of these tests is that the norm used as the basis for standardizing a test is that of the majority and that what the minority may wish to get out of college may be different from what the minority wants. For being different, the minority is classified as deviant, in terms of their scores on many standardized tests. All these are charges that should be investigated in depth.

Predictive Validity

With reference to whether or not these tests predict how well one may survive in school, the Educational Testing Services stated that numerous studies have given "definite support for the practice of using first-year [grade point] average as the criterion measure" (Schrader 1971, p. 118), and then it concluded, "the tests were almost invariably effective in predicting academic success" (Schrader 1971, p. 117).

I have both clinical and research information that casts doubt on the validity of standardized tests for minority students when predictive value has been determined by the first-year college grades of students. My study of black students at white colleges revealed that 52 percent of the black seniors had self-reported grades of A or B compared with only 42 percent of white seniors. During the same year in the public and private colleges that I studied, the black freshmen, sophomores, and juniors lagged behind whites in the proportion of As and Bs that they obtained. Indeed, the freshmen year was a near disaster for the black freshmen; only 14 percent of the blacks, compared with 47 percent of the whites, received grades that were good to excellent (Willie and McCord 1972, 86). These findings indicate that Scholastic Aptitude Test scores may be good predictors of the freshman year performance for whites and that their first-year performance is a good indication of their second, third, and fourth year performance, as several studies have shown (Schrader 1971, p 118); but this may not be the case for blacks. Note that only four percentage points separated the proportion of white freshmen from the proportion of white seniors with good to excellent grades, but thiry-nine percentage points existed between the black freshmen and seniors with grades at these levels. These data cast doubt on the assumption that the SAT score has the same predictive value for blacks as for whites in that black freshmen and seniors tend to exhibit academic performance behavior that differs considerably from the academic performance behavior of white freshmen and seniors as a group.

Moreover, during the course of my professional career I have advised black students who received low scores on standardized aptitude tests but high grades in their courses. One black student graduated Phi Beta Kappa, went on to law school, and did well. However, his law school admissions test score was in the 400s.

Although most behavioral scientists would accept the proposition that aptitude is inherited, they also believe that opportunity must be provided for its expression and the environment must cultivate its development. Failure to indicate whether the score an individual received is a function of heritability or uncultivated capacity or a blocked opportunity system is one of the limitations of aptitude tests.

More serious is the fact that "an aptitude test is concerned almost entirely with the future—with prognosis" (Garrett 1965, p. 142). Such tests "assess the traits believed necessary for success in . . . law" and other fields. However, "there is . . . little agreement as to what constitutes a 'competent' lawyer and practically no studies have been done on this subject" (Hart 1975, p. 397). The College Entrance Examination Board has recognized this fact but has done very little about it because of "a number of difficult problems in defining college success, especially if . . . the problem of college success [is tackled] in relation to life success." Among the problematical are "broad judgmental and philosophical issues" and "suitable measures of the qualities considered important" (Schrader 1971, p. 118).

According to Hart the question of whether or not the standardized tests such as LSAT are culturally biased has been raised "for more than a decade," but research in this area is difficult because of the small number of minority students in law school (1975, p. 396). For the great majority of law school students, the Law School Admissions Test clearly "predicts law school performance" (1975, p. 394). But validity studies "demonstrate that it would be unwise to admit students solely on the results they obtain on the test" (1975, p. 396); the applicant's undergraduate grade point average "is normally a better indicator of law school performance than is the LSAT" (1975, p. 397). The actual correlation between the test battery and law school grades is 0.50 (Garrett 1965, p. 160). This fact indicates that 75 percent of the variance in law school grades must be attributed to some source other than measured aptitude.

Considerable evidence refutes the predictive validity of aptitude testing for life-long success. According to Persell (1977, p. 61), David C. McClelland and others have mentioned this and many other limitations of standardized tests, "but they have been virtually ignored for almost 20 years." These tests, as indicated by Garrett (1965, pp. 153-154), "do not reveal *how* successful a [person] is likely to be over a long period of time in a profession," although they do provide clues.

The issues of values and goals of formal education, including those of minority and majority students, cries out for analysis. These issues have not been adequately addressed by the advocates of standardized testing, probably because the norms for the standardized tests are those of the majority. Most public policy makers, including the policy-making politicians and the research professors, assume that the educational goal of minorities is to be like the majority. A decade ago, James Coleman alerted educational leaders to the fact that an emerging definition of equality had to do with "effects of school . . . in terms of consequences of the school for individuals on *unequal* backgrounds and abilities." He said that in this definition, "equality of educational opportunity is equality of results given *different* individual inputs." Coleman warned educational leaders that such a definition taken in the extreme would imply that equality of educational opportunity is researched only when the results of schooling (achievements and attitudes) are the same for the average member of racial and ethnic minorities as for the average member of the dominant group (Coleman 1968, p. 104). Standardized testing for aptitude, achievement, and competency appears to be focusing only on outcome and does not consider input and process variables.

One educator has advanced two broad principles as the basis for student selection policies by a graduate school: "(1) selection should be such as to assure that the class is populated with individuals who themselves will enrich the educational experience of [the] school by their talents and viewpoints; and (2) selection should be designed to accept those who will best serve society upon graduation" (Hart 1975, p. 400). These two principles embrace diversity and service to society, which are worthy educational objectives. These principles recognize input, process, and outcome as variables that should influence admissions decisions.

My own professional experiences and review of the literature have demonstrated that minority and majority families want, need, and probably get different things out of formal education at all levels. Marie Peters (1976, p. 141) found that black parents rank honesty and truthfulness in their children as very important. This outcome can be classified as a moral goal of education that is as basic as the development of other skills. The case of Richard M. Nixon demonstrates this fact. By all measures Nixon had superior aptitude in communication and calculation skills, but he had to resign, according to Patrick J. Buchanan, assistant to the president, speech writer, and personal friend, because "[the president] hasn't been telling the truth to the American people. . . . The tapes [recordings of his conversations with staff members] make it evident he hasn't leveled with the country for probably eighteen months. And the President can't lead a country he has deliberately misled for a year and a half" (Woodward and Bernstein 1976, pp. 349-350).

The call for a broader definition of educational outcome as a criterion measure of the validity of standardized aptitude tests and their predictability has led to the development of a "general desirability measure" that includes characteristics in students that faculty members regard as significant and that are observable. This measure was developed by Junius Davis, published elsewhere, and summarized in the technical report on research and development activities relating to the Scholastic Aptitude and Achievement tests of the College Entrance Examination Board. "General desirability was an overall evaluation of the extent to which a student was 'the kind of student this institution should (or should not) admit' " (Schrader 1971, p. 119). Schrader reported that (1) intellectual quickness; (2) intellectual self-sufficiency and creativity; (3) intellectual interest; and (4) motivation to achieve correlated closely with the general desirability measure. This measure also correlated closely with such variables as honesty, open-mindedness, and altruism. To summarize, the faculty members affirmed that is is generally desirable to admit students who are intellectually gifted as well as honest and altruistic (Schrader 1971, p. 110). A study of these generally desirable students and their grades during the first year of college revealed that those who rated high on honesty, open-mindedness, and altruism did not always receive high grades.

Because minorities tend to believe that the development of the capacity to be honest is an important educational outcome, it very well could be that college does different things for different students. For students who enter with a well-developed sense of honesty and altruism, the college experience can be the means of maintaining these qualities and of improving their abilities in communication and calculation; for students who enter with well-cultivated verbal and computating skills, the function of college may be the maintenance of this capacity and the cultivation of ethical and moral methods of human interaction.

By limiting the criterion measure of the validity of the Scholastic Aptitude Test to first-year grades, that which majority freshmen bring to college is emphasized and that which minority students bring, which may be different, is ignored. Moreover, the extraordinary intellectual performance of minority seniors compared with majority seniors is ignored. On the basis of this analysis, one can better understand the charge by minorities of unfair treatment when admissions decisions to institutions of higher education are based on standardized aptitude test scores that do not measure what could be their unique contribution to a college community.

Complexities of the Learning Process for Minorities

Few researchers have taken into consideration the complexity of the learning process for minorities. Coleman and associates found that minority children in racially integrated schools achieve higher grades than minority children in racially segregated schools (Coleman et al. 1966). Irvin Katz's analysis of the Coleman data discovered that the "sense of control over fate and environment" was the most important attitude that contributed to "variances of verbal achievement" (Katz 1969, p. 68). Those blacks who have a stronger sense of control over what happened to them tended to achieve higher scores and to get better grades. Coleman's interpretation is that black children in integrated schools "gain a greater sense of their efficacy to control their destiny" very likely because "they see that they can do some things better than whites and can perform in school better than some whites, a knowledge which they never had so long as they were isolated in an all-black school" (Coleman 1968, p. 25). The testimony of Benjamin Mays about his experience at Bates College that was presented in chapter 3 also demonstrates this point.

On the basis of these data, one can understand why some black seniors outperform other blacks as well as whites, including white seniors. Very likely black seniors have a greater sense of their efficacy to control the college environment than either black freshmen, sophomores, juniors, or even white seniors, thanks largely to their developing over the years what W.E.B. Dubois has called "a double consciousness" (DuBois 1903)—viewing oneself as others see one, as well as having a sense of one's own identity and significance.

Function of Standardized Aptitude Tests

Then why use standardized aptitude tests at all, if they do not measure the full range of desirable characteristics in college students? A sociological analysis of their function in society is necessary. A macrosociological analysis should include but go beyond the charges of culturally biased examination questions, inappropriate criterion measures of test validity, limited educational goals, and narrow definitions of education. Such an examination should determine why a test is used that disproportionately excludes minorities from the student bodies of colleges and universities in a society in which education is a prerequisite for participating in many of its opportunities.

How such tests have been used in the past may provide some insight into why they continued to be used. Psychological testing first developed in Germany and France about the middle of the nineteenth century. Some of the earlier tests were for determining what a feeble-minded person could learn and how much and in what respects that person differed from the normal. For persons thought to be insane, tests were developed in years gone by to assess loss of memory, distortion of perception, distractability, and mental fatigue (Garrett 1965, pp. 5-6). Thus the first use of the tests was for separating those thought to be subnormal from the normal. It is fair to say that the tests have been used more to determine what to do with the less developed than to assist the people of exceptional talent. So far as admissions to educational institutions is concerned, standardized tests have been used largely to exclude.

In other instances, standardized tests have been used in education to obtain uniformity in the curriculum of different schools. The movement to organize the College Entrance Board in 1900 was sponsored by Nicholas Murray Butler of Columbia University and Charles W. Eliot of Harvard University. According to William Agnoff and Henry Dyer (1971, pp. 1-2), "At this time there was, in the opinion of the founders of the Board, appallingly little agreement among the colleges about the type of subject matter preparation and standards of proficiency required of the applicants." The Agnoff and Dyer study revealed that "many of the secondary schools and colleges regarded the movement toward uniform standards as a dangerous encroachment on their autonomy." In the end, however, the College Board with such powerful sponsorship won.

Today millions of young people participate in the annual testing program. The range of young people who go to college is much wider today than in 1926, when the first College Board Scholastic Aptitude Test was given, or even in 1941, when the students tested became the standardizing group for determining the scale "in terms of which scores on all future forms of the SAT would be expressed" (Agnoff and Dyer 1971, p. 3).

Yet the College Board has done little to develop a test that will assess the aptitudes of students who may have a different set of prioirities for college education."At the present time, as opportunities for post-secondary education are being widely extended to youths who in the past would not have been college bound, the Board through its Commission on Tests is re-examining its tests offering to see if they may be modified and extended to assess a wider range of talent" (Agnoff and Dyer 1971, p. 4).

The history of education in the United States has revealed the insidious nature of institutional discrimination, particularly of racism and elitism that exclude. Robert Merton published as essay on "The Self-Fulfilling Prophecy" that described the way the excluding process has operated. "[If] the dominant in-group believes that Negroes are inferior, and sees to it that funds for education are not 'wasted on these incompetents' and then proclaims as final evidence of this inferiority that Negroes have proportionately . . . [fewer] college graduates as whites, one can scarcely be amazed by this transparent bit of social legerdemain" (Merton 1949, p. 185). Because the proportions of blacks and other minorities who are graduating from high school and college have increased dramatically during the past decade, the criterion is rapidly shifting from possession of a diploma or degree as the basis for inclusion to performance on a standardized test. The affluent white and dominant people of power control the making, administration, and scoring of the tests. What we are witnessing then is institutional racism compounded by institutional elitism. This time poor and handicapped whites as well as blacks will be hurt by the faceless tests that exclude people from opportunities.

It seems to me that the standardized tests are but another barrier placed in the path of people who were not exposed to education in the past, but who are taking advantage of it more and more today, as was pointed out in chapter 1. Even though they have been awarded diplomas and degrees, the poor and racial minorities still are barred from opportunities formerly available to high school and college graduates until they reach predetermined scores on a standardized test.

Appropriate Assessment

Evaluation and assessment are appropriate. However, the persons best capable of assessing the performance of students are their teachers, peers, and colleagues. They are much more reliable than a faceless test that is prepared by people who are strangers to each other's way of life. Assessment should be based on a relationship.

Grades earned by students during their courses of study are sufficient indicators of their competence. If they are not, then the fault lies in the teaching, learning, and evaluation process. If this process is faulty, then it should be corrected. The standardized test places the blame on the student and protects the educational system. In the end, both student and the system lose when a mechanical assessment replaces an understanding human relationship.

The dean of the College of Letters and Science at the University of California at Berkeley is reported in the *New York Times* as saying that "too much emphasis [is] being placed on national standardized tests, the Graduate Record Examination and the law and medical school boards as a measure of a four-year undergraduate career" (30 May 1977, p. 6). The same may be said of other standardized tests of achievement and competency. Elsewhere, I have stated that "the poor and disadvantaged have some ideas of their own about what they would like to get out of formal education. These might include such goals as, for example, learning how to endure, how to develop a positive concept of the self, how to gain a measure of control over one's environment, how to transcend difficulty, and how to effectively deal with danger" (Willie 1973, p. 234). In the end, these skills have to do with survival for minorities. They too are skills that can emerge from a high school and college education. Minority students who learn survival skills in school obtain a beneficial education, even though they may not test as well as whites in science, mathematics, and reading. The standardized testing movement does not recognize that majority and minority populations may require both similar and different skills to cope with their unique circumstances.

Legitimizing Institutional Elitism

Finally, I believe that standardized testing is a disguised way of legitimizing institutional elitism and its excluding effects on the poor and oppressed. Joseph Gusfield has provided the theoretical framework for this portion of the discussion. His analyses of the American Temperance Movement as an experience in status politics is applicable to the standardized testing movement, which also is an experience in status politics. One can classify standardized testing as a form of social control.

It is important to analyze the standardized testing movement as a form of status politics and social control because it, like the temperance movement of yesteryear, has all the characteristics of "disinterested reform." Those who advocate use of standardized tests are not the parents of poor and oppressed young people and those who fail in school. They are the citizens who are affluent and well educated. Any "disinterested reform movement" ought to be carefully analyzed to determine what is the real self-interest of the reformers, which may be hidden from others and even from themselves by rationalization.

The education reformers who support the standardized testing movement do so, they say, as a way of maintaining academic excellence. Gusfield has found that so-called disinterested reform movements by the people of power and prestige are not so much for the benefit of the disadvantaged as they are for the purpose of preserving, defending, and enhancing the dominant people of power (Gusfield 1963, p. 3). Gusfield said that "the public support of one conception of morality at the expense of another enhances the prestige and self-esteem of the victors and degrades the culture of the losers" (Gusfield 1963, p. 5). The same may be said of the public support of one indicator of educational excellence over another.

When standardized tests are sanctioned by governmental institutions, they become the norm for all. Gusfield describes the process: "Since governmental actions symbolize the position of groups in the status structure . . . the individual finds in governmental action that his own perceptions of his status in the society are confirmed or rejected" (Gusfield 1963, p. 11).

Education is an important contributor to social status in the United States. Some, as mentioned earlier, have called it the fastest elevator to upward mobility. In the past, the proportion of people who graduated from high school and college was directly correlated with variations in social status—the higher the social status the greater the probability of being a high school or college graduate. Since the midpoint of the twentieth century, the proportion of racial minorities who have graduated from high school and college has increased greatly. Indeed, the proportionate increase for minorities and poor people has been greater than the proportionate increase for the majority and affluent people.

The call for standardized tests of competencies, aptitudes, and achievement by the dominant people of power is a subtle and symbolic way of putting down the less powerful and maintaining the control of the more powerful now that minorities are gaining on the majority in acquiring high school diplomas and the college degrees of respect.

Gusfield further states that "a more hostile attitude to reform is found when the object of the reformers' efforts is no longer someone he can pity or help" (Gusfield 1963, p.6). The militancy of the minority now evokes scorn rather than pity, and the standardized test is a new form of control of their uppity ways, which include aspiration for more education. Thus, standardized testing takes on new symbolic properties as a vehicle of status protest against those who could achieve the education of the dominant people of power. Finally, Gusfield states that "in the struggle between groups for prestige and social position, the demands for deference and the protection from degradation are channeled into government and into such institutions of cultural formation as schools . . . . Because these institutions have power to affect public recognition, they are arenas of conflict between opposing status groups" (Gusfield 1963, pp. 3-11). Thus, the standardized testing movement is appropriately identified as an aspect of status politics in the Unites States.

Doubt has been cast upon competency based testing for determining whether individuals should be awarded high school diplomas by recent reports of two federal government agencies. The March 1978 report of the National Academy of Education on *Improving Educational Achievement* stated that "any setting of state-wide minimum competency standards for awarding the high school diploma . . . is basically unworkable, exceeds the present measurement arts of the teaching profession, and will create more social problems that it can conceivable solve" (1978, p. iv). A January 1979 research report of the National Advisory Committee on Black Higher Education and Black Colleges and Universities, entitled *Access of Black Americans to Higher Education,* indicated who is likely to be harmed the most by this movement. Specifically, it said that "in instituting competency tests at the high school level, the onus and responsibility fall on the students" (1979, p. 9), and that "the new competency testing movement will likely be another barrier to full Black participation in higher education" (1979, p. xiii). Despite these warnings, at the close of the 1970s "approximately 36 states [had] some type of competency based education . . . underway" (1979, p. 8).

References

Agnoff, William H., and Dyer, Henry S. 1971. "The Admissions Testing Program." In *The College Board Admissions Testing Program,* pp. 11-13. Edited by William H. Angoff. Princeton: College Entrance Examination Board.

Coleman, James S., 1968. "Equality of Educational Opportunity." *Integrated Education* 6, no. 5 (September-October).

Coleman, James S., et al. 1966. *Equality of Educational Opportunity.* Washington, D.C.: U.S. Government Printing Office.

Daniels, Ralph S. 1977. *"Private Premises and Public Purposes: A State Defines Minimal Competencies."* A final project report presented to the faculty of the Graduate School of Education of Harvard University in partial fulfillment of the requirement of the degree of Doctor of Education.

DuBois, W.E.B. 1903. *The Souls of Black Folk.* Chicago: McClurg.

Garrett, Henry E. 1965. *Testing for Teachers.* 2nd ed. New York: American Book.

Gusfield, Joseph K. 1963. *Symbolic Crusade.* Urbana: University of Illinois Press.

Hart, Frederick M. 1975. "History and Organization of the Law School Admission Test and the Law School Admission Council." In *Hearings:*

Civil Rights Obligations, Part 2A, by the Committee on Education and Labor, U.S. House of Representatives. Washington, D.C.: U. S. Government Printing Office.

Horowitz, Irving Louis. 1972. "Qualitative and Quantitative Research Problems in Comparative International Development." In *Social Development,* edited by Manfred Stanley. New York: Basic Books.

Jerome, Judson. 1971. *Culture out of Anarchy.* New York: Herder and Herder.

Katz, Irwin. 1969. "Academic Motivation and Equal Educational Opportunity." In *Equal Educational Opportunity,* edited by the Editorial Board of the *Harvard Educational Review.* Cambridge, Mass.: Harvard University Press.

Merton, Robert K. 1949. *Social Theory and Social Structure.* New York: Free Press.

National Academy of Education. 1978. *Improving Educational Achievement.* Washington, D.C.: U.S. Government Printing Office.

National Advisory Committee on Black Higher Education and Black Colleges and Universities. 1979. *Access of Black Americans to Higher Education.* Washington, D.C.: U.S. Government Printing Office.

New York Times. 30 May 1977. "College Study Plans to Make Grades More Meaningful."

New York Times. 28 October 1977. "Jersey to Improve Civil Service Tests."

Persell, Caroline Hodges. 1977. *Education and Inequality.* New York: Free Press.

Peters, Marie. 1976. *"Nine Black Families, A Study of Household Management and Childrearing in Black Families with Working Mothers."* Ed.D. thesis, Graduate School of Education, Harvard University.

Remmers, H.H., and Radler, D.H. 1962. *The American Teenager.* Indianapolis: Charter Books.

Schrader, W.B. 1971. "The Predictive Validity of College Board Admission Tests." In *The College Board Admissions Testing Program,* pp. 117-144, edited by Henry Angoff. Princeton: College Entrance Examination Board.

Stanley, Manfred. 1972. "Introduction." In *Social Development,* edited by Manfred Stanley. New York: Basic Books.

Wilkes, Paul. 1977. *Six American Families.* New York: Seabury.

Willie, Charles V. 1973. "Perspective on Black Education and Education of Blacks." In *Does College Matter?* edited by Lewis C. Solmon and Paul J. Taubman, pp. 231-238. New York: Academic Press.

Willie, Charles V. and McCord, Arline. 1972. *Black Students at White Colleges.* New York: Praeger.

Woodward, Bob, and Bernstein, Carl. 1976. *The Final Days.* New York: Simon and Schuster.

6

On Selecting a Diversified Student Body

In American society, equality and equity are public service guidelines that apply to relationships in educational as well as economic, political, and other institutions. The courts have determined that a business available to the public cannot determine who should be its customers and exclude some persons in an arbitrary way. Goods and services in restaurants and common-carrier vehicles, for example, cannot be withheld from anyone willing to participate responsibly in the economic transaction through which the goods and services are rendered. The essential responsibility of a public school is similar: It is responsible for providing an adequate education to anyone of the appropriate age who is able to receive and use an education.

Some schools have a different perspective; they see their responsibility as that of offering whatever education they can provide to the best students available. Such a perspective is no different from that of white lunch-counter owners in the South before the age of desegregation. These owners believed that they had the right to offer their goods and services to whites only; they, of course, believed that whites were the best customers. Educational institutions including colleges and universities, like economic institutions, exist for the purpose of serving society. As public service agencies, they must make their goods, services, and opportunities available to any who need them and are willing and able to participate responsibly in the exchange process. Educational opportunities cannot be limited only to those who are classified as the best.

The truth-seeking capacity of a school would be severely impaired without students of varying existential histories, perspectives, and abilities. Moreover, any concept of the best is relative and tends to exclude in an unjustifiable way many who are capable or good enough. Elitism is no less damaging and harmful than other forms of oppression that exclude the full range of people who are necessary and essential in a well-functioning society.

An admissions process that is fair selects those students who are adequate and capable of receiving an education. This is what the medical school at the University of California did before the Bakke decision: it admitted a class of adequate students some of whom were more and less capable than others. All, however, were adequate and able. The white plaintiff in the Bakke case did not claim that he was the best student available for admission to the Davis campus of the University of California medical school. He merely claimed that he was more capable than some who were admitted, particularly the members of the minority population. He was silent on whether he was less capable than others who were accepted.

Random Selection

Many schools have applications from more students than they can admit. Under this condition, the fairest approach is to determine who is adequate and then to select in a random way from the pool of those who are adequate. If this approach were followed, the student body in all colleges and universities would be racially diversified and would be more or less similar to the proportions of various groups in the population at large, or, more precisely, to the proportions of the various racial groups among all adequate applicants.

Although a school need not give up its authority to determine admissions policies regarding the kinds of students most likely to be of service to society after participating in the educational process, it should keep the principles of adequacy and justice in mind in fashioning admissions policies. Whatever criteria are used should be fair; and the best way to guarantee that the selection process is fair is to admit students of different groups in proportions that are similar to their presence in the society at large or in the total pool of applicants.

It may be unfair when a population—whether minority or majority—is overrepresented in a student body. For this reason, the current concern about quotas is without merit, if the goal in admissions is to be fair. Any method of selection that results in a student body of adequate minority and majority individuals that is similar to the proportions of those groups in the population at large is fairer than any other method of selection. Rather than justify why adequate minority students should be included in a student body up to their proportion in the population at large by way of reserved spaces, as the University of California had to do in court, the burden of explanation and defense should be upon the majority. The majority population should be required to explain why its members are overrepresented when adequate minorities are available and the majority proportion of students is greater than it should be, if adequacy and justice were the criteria of selection.

Randomness can be set forth as a method for the fair selection of adequate students if it is assumed that there are no superior racial populations in the United States. This is the assumption of this discussion.

Critical Mass of Minority Population

Even when randomness is not used as a guideline, diversity should be maintained as an admissions goal. The fulfillment of this goal contributes to the creation of learning environments in which a majority population—that is, a majority in numbers—comes into contact with a minority population that is sufficiently large to have a social impact upon the total institution as a system.

Ideally, any group—black, brown, or white—that is the majority of the students should not be more than two-thirds of the total student body; and any group that is the minority should not be less than one-fifth of the total student body. The preferred ratio is a majority of not more than two-thirds and a minority of not less than one-third. When this cannot be accomplished because the minority students are too few in number, then the members of the minority present should be so clustered in some if not all of the schools so that they constitute at least one-fifth of the students in a particular institution.

The proportion of one-fifth seems to be the critical mass of a minority population that is necessary for the minority to have an educational impact upon the system and for the minorities to feel that they are not an oddity engaged in an experiment. The privilege should be available for students who are a majority to transfer to schools in which they would be a member of the minority, and for members of the minority to attend schools in which their presence would bring the critical mass of minorities up to at least 20 percent. These, however, are personal choices that should be available to all. At the level of planning and public policy, the ratios mentioned above are helpful guidelines.

The concept of a critical mass sufficient for a significant impact on a particular setting is important to keep in mind in achieving a desegregated student body. Any combination of minority groups is appropriate to reach the one-third preferred minimum.

This is the rationale for the proportions of minority and majority students that have been recommended. An identifiable racial population with a majority of not more than two-thirds of a student body must be compassionate not only toward members of the minority but also toward members of the majority. Otherwise, members of the majority might defect and jeopardize the controlling position of the majority. When the majority is greater than two out of every three, it tends to overwhelm the minority and be less sensitive to dissidents, even among the majority, who represent little, if any, real threat to the continuing dominance of the current people of power. Oppressive tactics are ever-present dangers and constant temptations for the many who dominate because their numbers are overwhelming. Thus, a student body of not more than two-thirds of any one racial population is a way of building in restraint and consideration on the part of the majority. These would appear to be valuable lessons for life in a democracy, and a desegregated school of the racial ratio recommended presents an opportunity for such learnings to take place.

Enhanced Education

One obvious purpose of student body desegregation is to enhance the education of students by facilitating the exchange of ideas between those who can teach each other problem-solving methods based on their unique cultural experience. This is why any combination of majority and minority students is appropriate, as long as no individual is excluded in an arbitrary and capricious way from any school. The particular racial minority with which the majority must deal is not important as long as the majority receives a desegregated education in the presence of a significant number of students dissimilar in some ways to the racial or cultural group that is in control.

It really does not matter which race is in the majority. As stated earlier, a majority of the students may be black, brown, or white in any school. There are assets and liabilities attached to majority and minority status. An important learning by minorities is how to trust and depend on others. Also, the continued participation in a situation that one does not control means that one must learn how to endure. Trust, endurance, and dependency are learnings that are valuable for whites, blacks, browns, and all people. Thus, whites ought to have the opportunity to obtain these learnings that are unique to the minority status and should be enrolled in some schools in which they are the minority, as mentioned in chapter 3.

Likewise, the majority learns some things that are unique to that status position—for example, the need to exercise restraint and compassion, as will be discussed in chapters 8 and 9. These learnings are beneficial for blacks and browns as well as whites. Thus, black and brown racial groups ought to be enrolled in some colleges and universities in which they are the majority but not an exclusive majority. They need to experience a desegregated education in the presence of a white minority so that they may learn how to behave with the compassion, consideration, and restraint of the majority. It is educationally sound for black, brown, and white students to experience minority status in school, and it is educationally sound for black, brown, and white students to experience majority status in school.

In summary, the student bodies in desegregated colleges and universities should be diversified rather than racially balanced. Whites need not always be the majority; blacks and browns need not always be the minority. The concept of diversity implemented according to the guidelines mentioned does two things: first, it prevents racial isolation in education, and second, it facilitates experiences for all of being in control or being dependent. This approach saves educators from being caught up in the numbers game of balancing racial populations. At the same time it protects against arrogant justifications for the disproportionate representation of any group. It identifies diversity as a genuine educational experience.

7 Enrollment and Retention of Black Students

The number of college-going black students increased from about one quarter of a million in 1955 to about a million and one-half in 1977 (U.S. Bureau of the Census 1960, p. 105; 1978, p. 160). As the 1970s closed, blacks were closing the educational gap between their population and that of whites.

The hundred or more historically black colleges could not accommodate this rapid increase in number of students. Thus, a larger proportion of black students in higher education began to enroll in predominantly white colleges and universities. In 1976, the year in which the United States celebrated its bicentennial anniversary, 64 percent or nearly two-thirds of all black students were enrolled in predominantly white institutions of higher education (U.S. Bureau of the Census 1978, pp. 160-161). This fact does not mean that predominantly black colleges and universities were losing students, since they educated an overwhelming majority of all blacks before the *Brown* case in 1954, and as many as half of all black students as recently as 1965. Actually their enrollment increased several fold between the year in which the *Brown* decision was rendered and the end of the 1970s.

Even though blacks have been closing the educational gap, much remains to be accomplished in achieving educational equity in higher education. For example, the National Association for Equal Opportunity in Higher Education reported that a higher proportion of college-going blacks receive baccalaureate degrees from predominantly black colleges (Willie 1978, p. 148). Because most blacks study in predominantly white colleges, the failure of these schools to sustain minority students through four years of the full course of study has resulted in an attrition rate that is alarmingly high.

In addition to a higher dropout rate for blacks in predominantly white schools, another concern is the inequitable distribution of blacks among two-year and four-year colleges as well as among postgraduate or professional schools and universities. During the bicentennial year, 11 percent of all students full-time enrolled in two-year colleges were black. The black population was only 8 percent of all full-time students in four-year colleges, and as low as 5 percent for all full-time students in graduate and professional schools. If racial equity in enrollment were present, 11 percent of the students at each level would have been black (National Advisory Committee on Black Higher Education 1979, p. 11).

The dropout rate for blacks in predominantly white colleges indicates that these schools are not doing all that they should do to retain racial minority students. There is no justifiable reason why the dropout rate for blacks in predominantly white colleges should be higher than the dropout rate for whites in these same schools. Also, the data on the distribution of blacks among different kinds of schools indicate the presence of selective processes that disproportionately excluded some racial populations.

In 1954, the year of the *Brown* desegregation court decision, the United States Office of Education classified 106 colleges and universities as predominantly black; these colleges enrolled seventy-five thousand students, with an average enrollment of about seven hundred. In 1976, that total had increased to 149 according to the National Center for Education Statistics (U.S. Bureau of the Census 1978, p. 161). These institutions enrolled three hundred eighty-one thousand students that year. Despite their value as places from which blacks tended to graduate at a higher rate than the predominantly white institutions, clearly these institutions could not carry the full load of educating all college-going students in the nearly four million blacks eighteen to twenty-four years of age (U.S. Bureau of the Census 1978, p. 29). Thus, the future of blacks in higher education, because of population size alone, will require their enrollment in predominantly white schools as well as in predominantly black colleges and universities.

Historically Black Colleges

In 1968, David Riesman and Christopher Jencks called black colleges collectively "academic disaster areas" and predicted that ambitious black students in the future would bypass these schools for predominantly white colleges and universities (Riesman and Jencks 1968, pp. 433, 417). The facts of the matter reveal that both their definition of black colleges and their prediction about the future enrollment of blacks were in error. The information provided by Prezell Robinson causes one to wonder how an honest assessment without malice could label black colleges "academic disaster areas." They have produced, according to Robinson, "about 85 percent of the black doctors, approximately 80 percent of black lawyers, and more than 70 percent of black elected officials" (Robinson, 1978, p. 158).

The increase from seventy-five thousand to three hundred eighty-one thousand students mentioned previously resulted in an average of around twenty-five hundred students per school for predominantly black institutions. Clearly, black students were not bypassing predominantly black colleges as Riesman and Jencks said they would. Moreover, an increasing number of white students were attracted to these historically black colleges. Toward the close of the 1970s, the estimated number of white students enrolled ranged from thirty-eight thousand to fifty-seven thousand. If the lower estimate of 10 percent of white enrollment is used, it yields an average of 255 white students per black college; the higher estimate of 15 percent yields an average of approximately 380 white students per black college. Black colleges have accepted whites, and they have accepted blacks who genuinely want to learn despite their previous preparation for higher education. In addition, they have provided a unique opportunity for whites to experience minority status. Further discussion of the adaptation of whites on predominantly black college campuses is presented in chapter 9.

In an article on "Black Colleges Redefined" that was published in the October 1979 issue of *Change*, I point out that "a higher education system with a Harvard but not a Hampton is incomplete" (Willie 1979, p. 49). In addition, our higher education system needs a Morehouse and a Miles. Diversity is the word. It is a self-correcting phenomenon. John Monro described the first-year students at Miles College and other open-door colleges:

> The freshman class ranges widely in ability, in previous training, in information, and in motivation. . . . Practically all our freshmen are invisible to the selective colleges. . . . The truth is—and all of us on the open-door campuses know this from experience—that a serious percentage of our "invisible" students are well above average in intellectual ability. . . . Based on what I see at Miles College, I would say that at least fifteen percent or twenty percent of the students entering open-door colleges are clearly able to handle demanding college work, given the chance (1978, pp. 235-236).

Monro contended that "our major colleges and universities are losing out on a large number of able students because these colleges do not know how to find them or work with them" (1978, p. 236).

Monro outlined four steps of concern: close scrutiny of what students bring with them to college, a program that deals with student needs in a firm but supportive way, a dedicated faculty interested in teaching students, and an academic management system that keeps tabs on what students are doing. He said that if a college will show such concern and undertake this kind of program, it will be richly rewarded in human results. With an affirmation of hope, Monro said, "Any college *can* do it. The problem is one of awareness, concern, and intent" (Monro 1978, pp. 235-237). If the pedagogical methods and techniques of black colleges became more widely known, other colleges could emulate them to their benefit, including, for example, Yale, Harvard, Vanderbilt, Wisconsin, Michigan, Berkeley, and others.

Academic Nurturance

Teacher dedication, of course, is not limited to black colleges, although the manifestation of it may be more widespread on such campuses than elsewhere. In his autobiography, *The Camera Never Blinks*, Dan Rather told about Hugh Cunningham, his journalism teacher at Sam Houston State. As Rather reported, his teacher took him under his wing, fed him periodically, and kept lining up part-time jobs for him. In addition to concern for his health, Rather's teacher captured and held his attention with the intensity that poured out of him. He was a teacher who knew that he could make "a tremendous difference" with his students and he did. Rather described Professor Cunningham as gifted, with a restless mind, and also as a person with a decency that is impossible to overstate. He gave himself to his students, saw potential in them, and tried to relate to them the way a father would. Dan Rather summed up his experience this way: "I never felt that I suffered for having attended Sam Houston. Among other reasons, I had opportunities that would not have been available at a larger school. One of them was the closeness that could develop with a professor like Hugh Cunningham. . . . He encouraged us to think and read and form opinions" (Rather, 1978, pp. 22-36).

The teaching methods of these kinds of individuals, frequently but not exclusively found on the black college campuses, should be studied and, if possible, emulated. These teachers work with all kinds of students and fulfill the basic educational values of providing equal opportunity to learn sometimes better than professors at the most prestigious universities.

It should be clear in light of the testimony by Dan Rather that the responsibility of teaching students of varying racial and social class groups who want to learn regardless of previous level of preparation is not limited to black colleges. Indeed, it can be done effectively by any institution. And it can be done effectively for all students.

Despite the recent hullabaloo of the widely announced recruitment programs, black students in large numbers at white colleges are still rare, as indicated earlier. The approximately twenty-six hundred predominantly white colleges and universities in the United States averaged about 275 black students per campus (U.S. Bureau of the Census, 1978). The student bodies of these campuses range from several hundred to over one hundred thousand. Thus, black students were less than 5 percent of the students on most predominantly white college campuses.

The reasons why a small number of blacks and other minorities enroll in predominantly white colleges and a disproportionately small number in these populations compared with the number that enter such schools graduate have little to do with intellectual capacity.

The way that black students are nurtured on predominantly white campuses has a great deal to do with the ease or difficulty of their adaptation. Benjamin Mays' description of his experience at Bates College in Maine from which he graduated in 1920 is illustrative:

I had read in the Bates catalogue that . . . soon after the opening of the college year the sophomore declamation contest would be held. . . . I made up my mind that I was going to try to win the contest at Bates. . . . Someone told me that Mrs. Fred Pomeroy, wife of Professor Pomeroy who was head of the Biology Department, was good in speech and drama. . . . I was taking a course in biology and asked Professor Pomeroy to find out whether his wife would train me for the contest. He assured me that she would be happy to help me and indeed she was most gracious in coaching me. Campus gossip had it that I could not hope to win because of my Southern drawl. . . . The rumor intensified my determination to win, and I did, by unanimous decision of the three judges. . . .

I have always been deeply appreciative when people did things for me that they were in no way obligated to do. I shall never forget Mrs. Pomeroy (Mays 1971, p. 56).

Benjamin Mays entered Bates College in September 1917. "During my first semester at Bates," he said, "I made only one A, and was embarrassed and chagrined to receive the first and only D in my whole academic career. . . . I was one of the fifteen to be graduated with honors." Later, Benjamin Mays was elected to Phi Beta Kappa.

Mays explained how he received that one A when he first enrolled in Bates:

Amusingly enough, that solitary A that graced my first semester record was made in Greek, the subject that was most difficult for me and troubled me most. . . . I had particular difficulty with pronunciation. . . . I can recall that once . . . I studied Greek until midnight and got up at three A.M. to study more. I asked Professor Chase for a conference to discuss the difficulty I was having. He invited me to his home, analyzed the problem, made some suggestions, and assured me that I had the ability to do the job. Immediately I begun to improve, and by the end of the semester I had made an A (1971, pp. 57-58).

This experience of receiving help and assurance when he needed it made a tremendous impression on Mays. In his autobiography, he said, "While President at Morehouse, I always urged every student to seek an early conference with his teacher if he was having difficulty with a subject" (Mays 1971, pp. 57-58).

Looking back upon his college experience in a predominantly white school, Mays said that "adjusting to a new physical and spiritual environment might well explain those low grades" the first semester. After that period, he said, "things had gone . . . well for me at Bates" (Mays 1971, p. 60).

The experiences of Dan Rather with Professor Cunningham at Sam Houston State and of Benjamin Mays with Mrs. Pomeroy and Professor

Chase at Bates College indicate that academic nurturance by sympathetic mentors is one of the chief causes of student success in college, and that good academic performance is an outcome of teacher effort as well as of student response. Black and other minority students and women tend to have difficulty in finding sympathetic mentors.

Trust

My study of black students at white colleges indicates that black students tend not to trust their white teachers. "Trust. That's the main word," said a group of blacks. "Black students need someone they can trust." I found that most of the black students at white colleges have never had a private conference with a teacher outside the classroom, that only about one-third believed that the teacher is the person with whom to register a complaint about grades, and that only one-sixth felt that the teacher could be turned to for academic guidance such as the choosing of courses and instructors.

A frequent complaint of black students at white colleges was that white teachers ignored them, that these teachers did not comprehend the black experience, and that they discouraged black students from discussing and researching their racial heritage as an educational exercise. Some white faculty members were described as hypocritical and patronizing. One black student summed up the collective sentiment of several students in these words: "What we need is for people to be honest with us" (Willie and McCord 1972).

Black students are as likely to go to the dean or another administrator as to a faculty member to register a complaint about an academic problem. White students are more inclined to take up such problems with their teachers. The blacks expect to receive more understanding from administrative officers and less cooperation from the faculty. However, the confidence of black students in white administrators is not overwhelming. Nearly one out of every two black students believed the administration to be intolerant too.

Because of the estrangement in race relations that has occurred over the years, black advisers and black faculty are essential on predominantly white college campuses if black students are to have any confidence in these institutions. In my study, black advisers on white college campuses were described as "someone you can talk to," "a source of information," "someone really concerned," "someone with whom you can identify," and "someone who can ease the pain a little bit." Black faculty and advisers are links of trust between black students and white schools until the two can learn to trust each other (Willie and McCord 1972). Although black students are deeply suspicious of the motives of teachers and administrators at white schools, they will participate in recruiting more blacks, as indicated in chapter 4. Other black students are a source of support in an untrustworthy environment.

A great impediment to the success of black students at white colleges is the tendency for white teachers too quickly to label black students as academically unable when they do not behave the same as white students. In my study, as mentioned in chapter 5, only about one-sixth of the black students in white schools received grades at the A and B level during their freshman year compared to slightly less than one-half of the white students. By the senior year, however, 52 percent of the black students had grades at the A and B level. This proportion was ten percentage points greater than the 42 percent of white students who had grades at the A and B level (Willie and McCord 1972, pp. 85-87). The black students in white colleges in my study adapted to their new physical and spiritual environment similarly to the way that Benjamin Mays adapted to his. What a waste for American civilization it would have been if Benjamin Mays had been discharged from Bates College because of his shaky start during his first semester.

The wisdom of the Bible is as applicable to education as it is to religion. In the book of Ecclesiastes it is written: "To everything there is a season, and a time to every purpose. . . . A time to plant, and a time to pluck up. . . . A time to keep silence, and a time to speak" (Eccles. 3:1-8). Black students tend to be silent during their first year in college because of the new physical and spiritual environment that they experience on the predominantly white college campus. In due season, they speak out. By their senior year, black students make a mighty effort that often surpasses the achievement levels of whites. They not only transcend their poor performance of the early college years; they truly overcome. The season for learning for black students may differ from that for white students. The acceptable season and tempo for whites should not be projected upon blacks if we are genuinely interested in retaining minority as well as majority students in our colleges and universities.

References

Mays, Benjamin E. 1971. *Born to Rebel*. New York: Scribner's.

Monro, John. 1978. "Teaching and Learning English." In *Black Colleges in America*, edited by Charles V. Willie and R.E. Edmonds. New York: Teachers College Press.

National Advisory Committee on Black Higher Education. 1979. *Access of Black Americans to Higher Education*. Washington, D.C.: U.S. Government Printing Office.

Rather, Dan. 1978. *The Camera Never Blinks*. New York: Ballantine Books.

Riesman, David, and Jencks, Christopher. 1968. *The Academic Revolution*. New York: Doubleday.

Robinson, Prezell. 1978. "Effective Management of Scarce Resource: Presidential Responsibility." In *Black Colleges in America*, edited by Charles V. Willie and R. E. Edmonds. New York: Teachers College Press.

U.S. Bureau of the Census. 1960. *Statistical Abstract of the United States*. Washington, D.C.: U.S. Government Printing Office.

_____ . 1978. *Statistical Abstract of the United States*. Washington, D.C.: U.S. Government Printing Office.

Willie, Charles V. 1978. "Uniting Method and Purpose in Higher Education." In *Black Colleges in America*, edited by Charles V. Willie and R.E. Edmonds. New York: Teachers College Press.

_____ . 1979. "Black Colleges Redefined." *Change* 11 (October):46-49.

Willie, Charles, and McCord, Arlene. 1972. *Black Students at White Colleges*. New York: Praeger.

Part III
Black Students and White Students

8 Black Students in Black Colleges and in White Colleges

As late as 1977, the proportion of white adults twenty-five years of age and over who had graduated from college (which was 16 percent) was twice as large as the proportion of black persons in this age category who had graduated from college (7 percent). A discrepancy this large at the highest level of educational achievement continued to exist between the races, although their median school years completed were similar—roughly twelve years for all persons compared with eleven years for black persons in the United States (U.S. Bureau of the Census 1978, p. 143).

Further evidence of the absence of equity between the races, despite some progress, were data about the kinds of schools in which blacks were enrolled. A study that was issued by the American Council on Education in 1974 revealed clearly the underrepresentation of blacks in universities that award graduate degrees. Of all persons enrolled full time or part time in pursuit of a master's or doctoral degree, less than 5 percent were black (National Board on Graduate Education 1976, p. 44).

This chapter will examine the instructional styles of predominantly black and of predominantly white colleges and universities and their impact upon blacks in higher education.

Black Students in Black Colleges

The census of black students in black colleges has risen over the years, largely because black students have found these colleges to be accepting schools that provide them with a unique education including survival skills for the experiences they must face in a racist society.

Curtis Banks, a psychologist, and his associates have indicated the probable reasons why black students continue to enroll in large numbers in predominantly black colleges despite the negative characterization of these schools by some white scholars: "The objectivity of negative evaluative responses from whites may be perceived as low." According to Banks and his associates, "The global conception of the devastating effects of negative social reinforcement upon blacks cannot be affirmed." Moreover, "certain cognitive processes which are likely to mediate the impact of any social evaluative information upon the individual appear in particular to provide a buffer for black persons against the negative feedback of white sources"

(Banks 1977, pp. 137, 143). In other words, blacks tend to discount the criticisms such as those advanced by Riesman and Jencks (1968, p. 317) as uninformed and without merit.

Black colleges and universities have pioneered in providing higher education for some young people who were thought to be outside the mainstream of American academic standards and have developed unique and extraordinary methods of instruction for students with special needs. They have done these things because they are flexible. Their flexibility has enabled them to combine classical and career education at a time when a growing number of white as well as black students are insisting that higher education should equip them with sufficient skills to get a good job upon graduation. The synthesis of liberal arts and vocationally oriented courses in the curriculum of black colleges and universities that was discussed extensively in chapter 1 has placed these institutions in the vanguard of higher education. This synthesis, as mentioned earlier, emerged out of the Booker T. Washington—W.E.B. DuBois debate at the beginning of the twentieth century on the nature of higher education appropriate for blacks.

Patricia Gurin and Edgar Epps found that the civil rights movement of the 1960s enabled black college students to achieve another synthesis—a union between collective achievement and self-assertion. They found that "some held on to high levels of personal aspiration for educational and occupational achievement and gained pleasure from meeting personal standards of excellence while they also worked persistently throughout their college years to improve the conditions of life for others" (Gurin and Epps 1975, p. 386). Gurin and Epps state that low-income black students who attend black colleges "do not present personality deficits so often assumed to result from cultural restrictions and deprivation." What they need, and what the black colleges have provided, are opportunities for talent development, experiences that reinforce their self-confidence, information, exposure, and models of educational and occupational achievement (Gurin and Epps 1975, p. 141).

In describing the first-year students at Miles College and other open-door predominantly black colleges, John Monro said (1978, p. 235ff), "The freshman class ranges widely in ability, in previous training, in information, and in motivation." It should be pointed out that not all black colleges are open-door colleges and not all open-door colleges are black.

Daniel Thompson told the Black College Conference at Harvard that "the work of talented, dedicated, persevering teachers has substantiated the claim of black colleges that they can take certain students who are rejected by most or all of the affluent, high-ranking, prestigious white colleges and produce a relatively large proportion of top flight college graduates." This can be done, Thompson pointed out, because "teachers in black colleges . . . are more concerned with classroom activities, personal counseling, sponsoring organizations" (Thompson 1978, pp. 182, 190). The faculty members in most black colleges and universities are oriented to teaching and counseling. The experience of black students on predominantly white college campuses is different from that described by Thompson.

Black Students in White Colleges

Studies indicate that the separatist movement of black students on many predominantly white college campuses is not merely a fad or something that will soon pass. With more interaction between the races on campus as the numbers of black students have increased, the level of trust between blacks and whites appears to have decreased. This may be due to an unmasking effect, which the increased interaction has produced. Most blacks who enrolled in white colleges, according to my study of four upstate New York schools, expected to find less prejudice, less discrimination, and more social integration than they actually encountered. Their confidence and trust in whites was shaken by cruel or, at the very least, thoughtless insults and insensitivity. For many blacks, these experiences were cause for anger and despair and contributed to their call for separation and withdrawal (Willie and McCord 1972). A few blacks at white colleges have sought reparations and revenge.

Because of this general lack of trust, many black students believe that they may turn only to other black students for help and social life. A considerable amount of separation, black from white, already has taken place in living arrangements. Most black students live with black roommates for most of their college careers. An increasing number in my New York State study expressed preference not only for black roommates but also for all-black sections within dormitories. The all-black dormitory, though much discussed, is not a preferred housing arrangement for most black students yet. The number of blacks who prefer a racially homogeneous black dormitory is slightly more than one-fourth; some students estimate that only about one-fifth would choose to live in such a housing facility. This proportion is the same as that of blacks who have lived only with whites on most predominantly white college campuses. Thus, a majority, or three-fifths, of the black students still prefer some kind of integrated living arrangement that is neither exclusively black nor exclusively white.

Because of their common experience of racial segregation on white campuses, many blacks who are forced upon each other for social life tend to begin their relationships with each other on a brother-sister basis. They tend to take each other for granted rather than cultivate relationships. Interaction becomes so intense that most relationships are treated as primary relationships, even those that probably would have remained impersonal and secondary in other circumstances. This means that many blacks on white college campuses act as if they have almost unlimited access to all other blacks—the brothers and sisters—such as might occur in a family. For some, this kind of social arrangement is comfortable and generates considerable security; for others, it is confining, oppressive, and sometimes exploitative.

That more blacks are being recruited in white colleges and that a number of white students want blacks on campus and want them to live in their midst in the dormitories should not be interpreted as a sign that black and white students are beginning to make common cause. Whites still have limited interest in racial problems that blacks experience on campus or in the community. Few discuss these kinds of issues with blacks.

Despite the successful performance of many fourth-year black students, they along with other black schoolmates doubt that they will be able to get good jobs commensurate with their education. A majority believe that chances are better today than they were some years ago, but a large minority are uncertain. Whether or not the hopes and aspirations of blacks are fulfilled depends in part upon the responses of whites. However, whites on the college campus and elsewhere in society are increasingly less willing to redress the grievances of blacks because they tend to believe that the racial situation is better than blacks say it is.

Summary

In summary, one might conclude that black students in black institutions have achieved a synthesis of classical and career educations that focuses on individual achievement and group advancement and that provides survival skills for life in a racist society. In this respect, the structure and process of education in black institutions of higher learning can be instructive for whites and for the majority who want a college education to enable them to get good jobs upon graduation.

Unfortunately, most investigations of black institutions analyze these schools as deviant organizations. This perspective causes many social-science analysts to overlook the innovative methods and approaches of these schols that are transferable. Moreover, black colleges seldom have been advocated as settings in which whites could learn how to function in a minority status. A few whites, however, have turned to them and are having this unique experience that will be examined in the next chapter.

The in-depth study of black students in white colleges and universities is a study in race and culture contact and provides many opportunities for testing social theories. White students on predominantly white college campuses tend to treat blacks as if they were invisible and insist that blacks conform to the norms of the majority. This orientation on the part of whites generates mistrust among blacks regarding the reasons why white institutions recruited them. The absence of trust, as this analysis has revealed, is a fundamental impediment to easy interaction between populations that are racially different.

A contribution of this analysis is the identification of *trust* as a legitimate and important sociological variable that affects all social organizations and that mediates the relationships and interaction among groups and individuals. The finding that trust between black and white students tends to decrease with increased contact and interaction on predominantly white college campuses can enhance our understanding of what to expect initially from the coming together of previously estranged populations. Such an understanding should prevent disillusionment when harmony does not appear immediately after desegregation.

References

Banks, W. Curtis et al. 1977. "Some Effects of Evaluative Feedback upon Compliance and Self-Evaluation in Blacks." In *Third Conference on Empirical Research in Black Psychology*, edited by William E. Cross. Washington, D.C.: National Institute of Education.

Gurin, Patricia, and Epps, Edgar. 1975. *Black Consciousness, Identity, and Achievement*. New York: Wiley.

Monro, John. 1978. "Teaching and Learning English." In *Black Colleges in America*, edited by Charles V. Willie and R.E. Edmonds. New York: Teachers College Press.

National Board on Graduate Education. 1976. *Minority Group Participation in Graduate Education*. Washington, D.C.: National Academy of Science.

Riesman, David, and Jencks, Christopher. 1968. *The Academic Revolution*. New York: Doubleday.

Thompson, Daniel. 1978. "Black College Faculty and Students." In *Black Colleges in America*, edited by Charles V. Willie and R.E. Edmonds. New York: Teachers College Press.

U.S. Bureau of the Census. 1978. *Statistical Abstract of the United States*. Washington, D.C.: U.S. Government Printing Office.

Willie, Charles V., and McCord, Arline. 1972. *Black Students at White Colleges*. New York: Praeger.

White Students in Black Colleges

The Southern Regional Educational Board authorized in 1977 a study of whites in predominantly black public colleges and universities (Standley 1978). The principal investigator was Nancy V. Standley of Florida A. and M. University, a predominantly black public institution of higher education. The study included twenty predominantly black schools all located in the South in which approximately 10 percent of graduate and undergraduate students enrolled were white. The study analyzed the attitudes and self-reported experiences of white students regarding the campus climate and learning environment, including interpersonal relations. The study also obtained information regarding the white students' assessment of the competence of their teachers and of the adequacy of the curriculum, facilities, and support services in their schools (Standley 1978, p. 3).

Data and Method

The twenty southern colleges and universities with predominantly black student bodies were requested to distribute a questionnaire to a sample of one-fourth to one-third of all whites enrolled. Institutions with a white enrollment of less than 100 were asked to include all their white students in the study. A total of 2,550 questionnaires were distributed; 1,189 were returned. This number represented a return rate of 46 percent (Standley 1978, p. 24).

The research instrument consisted of a series of questions regarding the campus learning environment that required a response on a Likert-type scale: strongly agree, agree, undecided, disagree, strongly disagree.

Percentages were computed for the range of responses to each questionnaire item and published in the monograph that presented an initial analysis of the data (Standley 1978, pp. 36-39). This chapter presents a reanalysis of these data and further interpretation. The data on which this analysis is based may be found in the appendix to this chapter.

These are some of the characteristics of the students who responded. Seven out of every ten were born in the South, and a similar proportion attended predominantly white high schools. They were older than most college students; indeed, eight out of every ten were twenty-three years of age or over. A majority (about 60 percent) were married. Almost all lived off campus. They attended day classes (56 percent) and evening and weekend classes (44 percent). Three to four out of every ten of the white students were enrolled in a graduate course. Most were performing well at the B level or above. Education was the field in which a majority majored; it was followed by the natural sciences, the social sciences, and business. Of these white students, 41 percent were male and 59 percent were female (Standley 1978, pp. 30-35).

Findings

First, we attempted to determine areas of greatest uncertainty for white students in predominantly black colleges and universities. Extracurricular activities created the most uncertainty. A majority of the white students questioned whether student government on campus adequately represented their point of view and were uncertain as to whether they were welcome to participate in campus politics.

Also the white students were undecided about whether interracial dating was acceptable, and they could not quite make up their minds whether they found the campus musical events appealing and entertaining. If such events were not entertaining, then white students could justify not attending these extracurricular functions.

Extracurricular activities are less predictable and can foster random intimacy. Harvey Molotch's study of managed integration in the South Shore area of Chicago discovered that there is great inhibition to random intimacy in most urban settings. Molotch found that people tend to shy away from intimate contexts in which there is uncertainty of the trustworthiness and acceptance of others. He found that people tend to feel interpersonal vulnerability in uncontrolled social situations (Molotch 1972, pp. 177-184). Even in religious organizations such as churches, Molotch found that integration existed primarily in terms of formal worship, where the role relationships were prescribed and predictable, and less so in the social-life activities of the church outside of worship services. Social activities were virtually completely segregated in the integrated community that he studied.

The white students on predominantly black college and university campuses exhibited great uncertainty particularly about social events. Their uncertainty probably reflected interpersonal vulnerability and fear of rejection. Molotch said that interpersonal vulnerability is an important determinant of racial patterns (Molotch 1972, p. 190). Apparently the black students on predominantly black campuses had not yet given sufficient signals of acceptance to their white schoolmates to minimize their feelings of social vulnerability (Molotch 1972, pp. 198, 184).

The other area in which a majority of the white students on predominantly black college and university campuses expressed uncertainty had to do with personal services. Nearly six out of every ten remained undecided as to whether the counseling and advising services were especially sensitive to the needs of white students. Most white students enrolled in these predominantly black schools were not affluent (only one-third were members of families whose annual income was above the national median); yet they were uncertain whether financial assistance was readily available to them at the predominantly black schools. How much of the uncertainty could be attributed to fear of rejection if they had applied for financial assistance and been refused, and how much was due to reluctance to discuss personal money matters with college-staff members of a racial group that is considered to be a stranger to whites could not be determined from these data. An indication that some of the professional personnel in predominantly black institutions were looked upon as strangers is the high proportion (46 percent) of the white students who said that they were reluctant to use school health services because there were no whites or few whites on the staff. Whereas a similar proportion of white students (48 percent) were not reluctant to go to the campus health clinic, the high proportion who were reluctant to do so is mentioned because their behavior may be part of a pattern of tending to seek like-kind from whom to obtain personal services. The practice is found among blacks in predominantly white settings and among whites in predominantly black settings. In due time, such reluctance may pass away as the black and the white strangers become friends and learn to accept and trust each other. For the nonce, however, race still is a barrier to the revelation of intimate concerns for a large number of whites in predominantly black schools.

Helen Hughes and Lewis Watts studied blacks who moved into white suburbs in the Boston metropolitan area and found that "with astonishing rapidity the self-integrators' lives [took] on the character and tempo of the white suburbanites all about them" (Hughes and Watts 1970, p. 121). Yet several of these families returned to inner-city black ghetto communities for personal services such as legal, dental, and hairgrooming services. These neighborhood self-integrators who are black are not unlike the school self-integrators who are white.

There is a great deal of uncertainty among white students on black campuses concerning what is expected of them and why they chose these schools. The uncertainty tends to vanish with reference to specific learning experiences. When one discussed behavior in general (what is appropriate and inappropriate) and abstract reasons why one enrolled in one or another school, uncertainty reappeared regarding the choices that white students made.

For example, about 25 percent of the white students said that many black students expected them to adapt to the way of life of blacks; moreover, they felt that blacks on predominantly black campuses made less effort to adapt to others. A slightly higher proportion (about 30 percent of the white students) said that they disagreed with this assessment, and 45 percent were uncertain about how blacks expected them to adapt.

Whites also were unable as a group to state decisively why they had enrolled in a predominantly black school. About one-third said that whites would not have enrolled in such a school if there had not been special programs that attracted whites. Another one-third, however, said that this was not true, that regardless of the programs offered, whites would have enrolled. Still another one-third was uncertain as to whether whites would or would not have enrolled in a predominantly black institution without special reasons.

So new is the experience of racial integration, especially of whites enrolled in predominantly black colleges and universities, that the participants somehow feel that they have to justify their actions. The data show that there is little, if any, consensus among whites as a group regarding why they are present on predominantly black campuses. They probably have been attracted to such campuses for many different reasons. Even though it is true that about one out of every three whites enrolled because of the special offerings of a school, two out of every three are there for other reasons.

Despite the uncertainties, white students on black college and university campuses have derived some important educational benefits. Their most important learnings are that black schools provide a good education, that teachers in these schools help all students and are not partial because of the race of a student, and that the courses that the schools offer can contribute to future job plans.

Beyond specific educational opportunities that may contribute to future employability, the white students enrolled in black colleges and universities have learned a great deal about race relations in this nation. Through their regular social contacts with blacks on the campuses, 80 percent or more of the white students stated that they now have no difficulty communicating with a person of a race that is different from their own. Moreover, through such communication they have learned about the aspirations of blacks, have dismissed old racial stereotypes from their thinking, and have overcome the tendency to deny that prejudice continues to exist. They no longer are apologists for the status quo.

The negative concepts that have been eliminated from the information reservoirs of white students who have attended black schools have been replaced with positive concepts. Of the white students, 75 to 80 percent said that their education on black campuses have heightened their appreciation of different ways of life and caused them to be more concerned about equal opportunity for all. Moreover, they felt that their multiracial, multicultural experiences would help them to be more effective in their careers. These statements indicate that the white students found their education to be liberating and at the same time job-related. The provision of a "career-oriented education in a liberal arts context" is a typical expression used by black college presidents in describing the unique function of their schools (Willie and MacLeish 1978, p. 138).

The white students claimed that they received the comprehensive kind of education described because of a combination of factors. They said faculty on black college and university campuses were highly competent, students were educationally and vocationally motivated, and the campus atmosphere was one of tolerance. Such a setting was conducive to a range of experiences. Whites who attended black schools learned some things that were both similar to and different from what they could have learned on predominantly white college campuses.

Being a minority on black campuses, whites saw themselves for the first time in a different way. They said that they gained a better understanding of their own unique personhood. They developed what W.E.B. DuBois has called "a double consciousness"—the property of knowing who one is but also recognizing oneself in terms of how others see one. As discussed in chapter 1, the development of a double consciousness is a survival strategem for those in a less powerful status (DuBois 103, p. 3). DuBois explained that blacks had to learn the life style of whites as well as their own in order to survive. On the black college and university campuses, whites have had to learn the life style of blacks as well as their own. Learning how blacks perceived them helped whites to see themselves in a uniquely different way.

Coming face to face with the consequences of subdominant status, whites on predominantly black campuses recognized the negative effects of having too few people of one's own group on location. In fact, seven out of ten said that the presence of white faculty members and other white students on predominantly black campuses helped one feel as though one belonged. The white students were very aware of the need for a sufficiently large number of whites to facilitate increased participation by whites in the affairs of the school. The proportion of whites on the campuses of the institutions studied was 10 percent. Presumably this percentage was not sufficient. The white students were not sure that they could count on the administration to lead in efforts to break down racial barriers. If they had to rely on themselves, more white students were needed. Four out of every ten whites were uncertain as to whether the administration on the black college campus was making a genuine effort to recruit more nonblacks; 36 percent said the administration was trying to recruit more whites; 43 percent were undecided; 21 percent said the administration was not making genuine recruiting efforts.

Other studies have reported that when the subdominant population on a campus is too small, that group is condemned to "an inadequate social life and intraracial as well as interracial discord" (Willie and McCord 1972,

p. 15). Of the subdominant population, studies note that a school "should enroll a large enough number to ensure an adequate social life and educational experience." There should be enough students present to provide "a range of potentially compatible personalities and social types. Also the number should be sufficiently large so that all need not be known to each other personally. The goal is to have enough . . . students to provide freedom in association, flexibility in movement, and anonymity when desirable" (Willie and McCord 1972, p. 109).

The court-appointed masters in the Boston school desegregation case said that "whites need not always be the majority in good schools." Where whites are not the majority, however, they should be "a sufficient minority" to have a meaningful impact upon the system. From my own studies, as mentioned in chapter 6, I have determined that "the participation of less than one-fifth for a specific group in a democratic . . . organization is tokenism and tends to have little effect upon its decision-making structure." Thus, I conclude that "20 percent is the lower limit in terms of critical mass for a particular group" (Willie 1978, p. 20). The proportion of whites in predominantly black colleges and universities can be significantly increased over the years to the benefit of both black and white populations.

Summary

In summary, the study of whites on predominantly black college and university campuses that was sponsored by the Southern Regional Educational Board revealed that whites were receiving a career oriented and liberal arts education by competent teachers who cared about their students. Moreover, these whites had learned how to communicate with blacks. These experiences had increased multicultural knowledge for whites and heightened their sense of the need for equality of opportunity for all. Even though the white students were pleased with their new experiences, especially those that flowed from their subdominant status on campus, they wished that the schools would recruit more whites and that extracurricular and social encounters were as comfortable as their educational experiences. White students on predominantly black college and university campuses like their teachers and believe that they are getting a good and relevant education, but they have doubts about the sincerity and intentions of the administrators of these schools.

References

DuBois, W.E.B. 1903. *The Souls of Black Folk*. Chicago: McClurg.
Hughes, Helen MacGill, and Watts, Lewis G. 1970. "Portrait of the Self-

Integrator." In *The Family Life of Black People*, edited by Charles V. Willie. Columbus, Ohio: Merrill.

Molotch, Harvey Luskin. 1972. *Managed Integration*. Berkeley: University of California Press.

Standley, Nancy, V. 1978. *White Students Enrolled in Black Colleges and Universities*. Atlanta: Southern Regional Educational Board.

Willie, Charles V. 1978. *The Sociology of Urban Education*. Lexington, Mass.: Lexington Books, D.C. Heath and Co.

Willie, Charles V., and MacLeish, Marlene Y. 1978. "Priorities of Presidents of Black Colleges," In *Black Colleges in America*, edited by Charles V. Willie and R.E. Edmonds. New York: Teachers College Press.

Willie, Charles V., and McCord, Arline S. 1972. *Black Students at White Colleges*. New York: Praeger.

Appendix 9A: Selected Survey Items and Responses

Table 9A-1
Uncertainties of Whites on Black Campuses

	Response by Percent				
Items	*Strongly Agree*	*Agree*	*Unde-cided*	*Dis-agree*	*Strongly Disagree*
1. The student government here effectively represents my point of view	3.1	10.3	71.3	10.9	4.5
2. The musical events on this campus are appealing and entertaining	5.4	21.4	64.6	5.0	3.6
3. Most of the domitories on this campus appear to be well kept	2.4	23.4	59.5	10.0	4.6
4. I find that the counseling and advising services here are especially sensitive to the needs of white students	3.9	16.4	58.9	17.0	3.9
5. Interracial dating appears to be an acceptable social relationship on this campus	1.2	6.2	58.6	19.2	14.8
6. The campus political structure does not welcome white student participation	4.6	11.4	56.3	20.8	6.8
7. Financial assistance seems to be more readily available here, especially for me	9.8	18.5	50.5	12.1	9.0
8. Most of the people brought to the campus for lectures are stimulating and interesting to me	7.8	35.1	46.7	8.0	2.4
9. I am reluctant to use the services of the health clinic at this school because there are no (or few) whites on the staff	1.3	4.0	46.1	28.4	20.3
10. Many of the black students want the white students to adapt to them; the black students make less effort to adapt themselves to others	4.8	19.8	45.2	25.7	4.4

Table 9A-1 *(continued)*

	Response by Percent				
Items	Strongly Agree	Agree	Unde-cided	Dis-agree	Strongly Disagree
11. White administrators and white faculty members appear to have their input in the governance of this school	8.8	34.5	44.1	8.7	4.0
12. I feel that the overall admini-stration of this campus makes a genuine effort to recruit nonblack students	8.1	28.4	42.6	15.9	5.0
13. There appears to be sufficient and effective security on the campus to make me feel safe	12.3	50.3	42.4	7.9	5.1
14. I feel a real part of the school spirit	4.1	21.2	40.4	25.8	8.5

Source: Nancy V. Standley, *White Students Enrolled in Black Colleges and Universities: Their Attitudes and Perceptions* (Atlanta: Southern Regional Education Board, 1978), pp. 36-39 Reprinted by permission.

Table 9A-2
Positive Experiences of Whites on Black Campuses

	Response by Percent				
Items	Strongly Agree	Agree	Unde-cided	Dis-agree	Strongly Disagree
1. Most of my instructors do not show any partiality to students on the basis of race	45.9	43.0	4.0	5.9	1.3
2. My courses/educational experiences are closely tied to my future job plans	34.1	51.1	9.8	3.9	1.1
3. I have no difficulty communicating with black students on the campus	26.0	57.5	8.9	6.1	1.5
4. The things most blacks want is the same as what every other American wants: a chance to get some of the "good things of life"	29.5	54.2	11.9	3.0	1.3
5. A student's race does not affect his/her ability to learn	51.1	37.3	6.7	3.4	1.5
6. My social contacts on campus include both whites and blacks	28.0	54.2	10.6	5.6	1.5
7. In spite of all of the progress in recent years, there is still a great deal of prejudice operative in our society	26.9	52.8	10.3	8.2	1.8
8. My educational experiences here have given me a keener appreciation of different philosophies, cultures, and ways of life	25.1	53.7	13.6	6.3	1.3
9. I am not reluctant to tell people I go to school here	30.1	47.4	7.3	10.4	4.8
10. The cross cultural-multiracial experiences I am having here will make me more effective in my future career	25.7	52.6	15.9	4.4	1.4
11. Having a degree from here will not deter me from getting a satisfying "good" job	21.9	54.9	18.6	3.6	1.8
12. In most instances, on this campus, there is an atmosphere of tolerance and understanding of people and their views	13.6	63.0	16.8	5.0	1.5
13. Being a student here has made me more positively concerned about equal opportunities for all people, especially in education and careers	20.1	54.3	13.8	6.5	0.8

Table 9A-2 *(continued)*

	Response by Percent				
Items	*Strongly Agree*	*Agree*	*Unde-cided*	*Dis-agree*	*Strongly Disagree*
14. My family supported my decision to attend this school	17.6	54.9	16.0	7.8	3.7
15. The faculty members on this campus do demonstrate a high level of competence in their academic specialities	18.7	52.1	17.9	8.1	3.2
16. Most black students in my classes appear to be motivated toward developing themselves educationally and vocationally	17.5	53.1	14.4	10.8	4.3
17. The presence of white faculty members and other white students on the campus helps me feel like I belong	15.2	55.4	15.6	11.7	2.1
18. My educational preparation here has met my expectations	18.1	51.5	13.5	12.0	5.0
19. I feel uncomfortable when black instructors relate subject matters to activities and experiences of the black community and culture with which I have no familiarity	3.3	12.2	14.8	48.4	21.4
20. Most of the faculty of this campus are well qualified both by academic training and experience	18.0	50.9	20.6	7.7	2.7
21. Being a student here has given me the opportunity to understand and appreciate my own unique personhood	17.0	50.5	23.6	7.2	1.7

Source: Nancy V. Standley, *White Students Enrolled in Black Colleges and Universities: Their Attitudes and Perceptions* (Atlanta: Southern Regional Education Board, 1978), pp. 36-39 Reprinted by permission.

**Part IV
Black Colleges and
White Colleges**

10 Characteristics of Faculties in Predominantly Black and Predominantly White Colleges

Publicly supported colleges have received most of the increased number of black students recently enrolled in institutions of higher education. "Between 1970 and 1974, a 56 percent growth in college enrollment was noted for blacks, whereas white enrollment increased by only 15 percent" (U.S. Bureau of the Census 1975, p. 3). In 1974, 288,200 students were enrolled in the 120 predominantly black institutions in the United States. This number was about half of all blacks enrolled in college that year. In public two-year and four-year predominantly black colleges there were 197,300 black students, or about 38 percent of all blacks enrolled in higher education (U.S. Bureau of the Census 1977, p. 155). Thus, nearly four out of every ten blacks enrolled in college received an education in a predominantly black publicly supported institution.

The attendance pattern of black students in predominantly black institutions may be summarized this way: a majority of students in these institutions of higher education are in four-year schools; and of the students in black four-year colleges or universities, a majority are in publicly supported schools located in the South.

Christopher Jencks and David Riesman, in their article on "The American Negro College" published in 1967, characterized "the great majority of Negro institutions" as standing "near the tail end of the academic procession" (1967, p. 24), and said that "public Negro colleges are for the most part likely to remain fourth-rate at the tail end of the academic procession" (1967, p. 59).

Jencks and Riesman would not rate any black institution above "the middle of the national academic procession." Even at the midpoint, they ranked only "a handful of well-known private institutions . . . and an even smaller number of public ones" (1967, p. 25). Jencks and Riesman did not think well of black colleges in general and of publicly supported black colleges in particular.

The assertions of these two social scientists about public black colleges differ from those of others. For example, Daniel Thompson identified thirty-two public black colleges in 1973 and said that "with heavier appropriations, during the 1960s some Black state colleges assumed an image

By Gregory Kannerstein, Charles V. Willie, and Susan L. Greenblatt. Reprinted with permission from *Cross Reference*, no. 2 (March-April):97-105.

of vitality and academic responsibility" (1973, p. 42). He attributed the "aura of permanence" and "academic respectability" to court-ordered school desegregation. Because of this demand, "southern legislators began to appropriate increasingly large sums of money to support public Black colleges. . . . This marked a significant turning point in the development of Black higher education" (Thompson 1973, p. 42). Thompson further said that "during the 1960s, Black state colleges attracted a larger and larger number of high school graduates," especially those with "special talents" (1973, p. 43).

Jencks and Riesman admitted that more money had been pumped into predominantly black state colleges but contended that "the institutions will have an extremely difficult time competing for competent faculty" despite their recent affluence. They concluded that public black colleges "have very little to tempt a talented professor" (1967, p. 58).

A social scientist who has attended, taught in, and been an administrator of predominantly black colleges, Thompson has provided information counter to the arguments of Christopher Jencks and David Riesman. However, the public seems to have accepted the definition of the situation at public black colleges provided by the Harvard-based professors rather than that provided by a Southern-based educator. Since publication of these ideas, Riesman stated in a letter to one of the authors dated March 14, 1978 that "much of what was said seemed to both its authors mistaken and only shortly after it was published." However, as late as 1976, it could be said that "despite their unique educational programs, black colleges and universities have yet to be fully recognized for the value they have added to our national life. The belief that black colleges should be abolished which was covertly expressed at the beginning of the [1970] decade is now being openly advocated" (Willie and MacLeish 1976, pp. 95-96).

In 1970, the NAACP Legal Defense Fund and the Washington law firm of Rauh and Silard filed a class-action suit charging that the federal government had not enforced the Civil Rights Act of 1964 because dual higher educational systems had been permitted to continue in several states. The plaintiffs won that case in *Adams* v. *Richardson* in 1974. The Court required the federal government to obtain desegregation plans from ten states and to notify these states within a specified period of time whether or not the plans were acceptable.

In many instances, state plans filed with the Department of Health, Education, and Welfare gave the predominantly black colleges "the dubious distinction of bearing the chief burden of desegregation" (Pressley 1978, p. 7). Reporter Sam Pressley found this even in a northern state such as Pennsylvania.

The NAACP Legal Defense Fund had insisted that "since blacks did not create the dual system and [had] not been responsible for racial exclusiveness [that] the burden for dismantling dual systems and eradicating discrimination [should] not fall [disproportionately] on the victims . . . [the] black public colleges'' (Pressley 1978, p. 7). The desegregation plans of most states initially filed but rejected by HEW did not follow this guideline.

Charles U. Smith, a professor of sociology in a predominantly black school in Florida, has stated, with reference to the fact that many of the black state-supported colleges and universities are located in the same cities as are state-supported white institutions, "when the press reports on the feasibility and functioning of black and white institutions in the same city, the releases almost invariably state or imply a threat to the survival and development of the *black* school only'' (1978, p. 209).

In 1972, for example, the federal court ordered the state of Tennessee, among several alternative actions, to "consider the feasibility of a merger or consolidation of [Tennessee State University] and [the University of Tennessee at Nashville].'' In response to this order, the state of Tennessee "file[d] an interim plan for increasing the white presence on TSU's campus,'' the predominantly black state-supported school. This plan was rejected because, the court said, it placed a disproportionate burden of desegregation upon the victim of the dual system of higher education and would permit the predominantly white state-supported campus [UT-N] to remain overwhelmingly white. In the *Gier* v. *Blanton* decision of the U.S. District Court in 1977 the two campuses were ordered to merge, with Tennessee State University—the predominantly black campus—as the home campus.

The Tennessee case is of particular interest from two perspectives. First, it indicates that when most state authorities are required to desegregate colleges and universities, their first effort is to eliminate the predominantly black schools. Second, it indicates that a predominantly black school had been found, finally, by a judicial authority as worthy of becoming the home base in a merger with a predominantly white school. The Court found that the predominantly white institution, the University of Tennessee in Nashville, was "a newly created branch'' and that "neither the record nor the historical facts would support placing the merged institution under the University of Tennessee Board of Trustees.'' With referencce to the predominantly black institution, the Court found that it was "a land-grant university with a 60 year history'' and that for the Board of Trustees of the University of Tennessee to take over the merged institution would mean "the elimination of Tennessee State University as an educational institution with all the concomitant losses entailed therein.''

Methods and Data

The purpose of this study is to analyze some of the losses that would result if predominantly black colleges and universities sharing a common city with predominantly white colleges and universities were closed. Seldom has there been a comparative analysis of the quality of predominantly black and predominantly white institutions of higher education. The United States District Court in the *Geier* v. *Blanton* case conducted a limited analysis, but it is the responsibility of social scientists to do this in a more systematic way. We have, therefore, analyzed comparatively white colleges and universities located in the same community. The faculties were chosen because the instructional staff is the heart of an educational institution, and public colleges were analyzed so that the source of financial support would be similar and held constant.

According to Jane Smith Browning, there are fourteen areas in the United States in which black and white public colleges are located close together (1975, p. 49). Nine of these pairs are in the same cities. For the schools in five of these cities, it was possible to acquire information regarding the academic background of the faculties. The cities studied are shown in table 10-1.

Characteristics of the faculty were obtained from information printed in the most recent college catalogue that was available. Six of the ten schools in the study had catalogues dated 1976; two were dated 1975 and two, 1974.

Faculty were analyzed in terms of size; college or university awarding academic degrees; racial composition of the school from which academic degree was received (including domestic or foreign location of the school); the type of degree received—that is, bachelor, master, or doctoral; and whether or not the faculty person was a graduate of the school at which he or she was teaching. A few faculty members in the performing arts did not have college degrees. They were not included in the study. A few faculty members with law degrees were included, and their degrees were tabulated as doctorates.

In the five predominantly black publicly supported colleges and universities, there were 1,303 faculty members. The publicly supported five white institutions had a total of 1,605 faculty members.

Table 10-1 presents information about the general characteristics of the ten institutions included in the study. All ten are state-supported schools and have academic programs at both the undergraduate and graduate levels. The two institutions in Savannah jointly sponsor graduate programs; all of the other graduate and undergraduate programs are independent.

All the institutions may be classified as small to medium in terms of size of student body. The smallest is Savannah State, with just over 2,500 students, and the largest is University of North Carolina at Greensboro with 9,409 students. The average size student body is 4,874.

An interesting point to note is that four of the five black colleges are older than their white counterparts, and the fifth, North Carolina Agri-

Table 10-1
General Characteristics of Predominantly Black and Predominantly White Institutions

City—University	Year Founded	Type of Institution	Faculty	Students
Baltimore, Maryland Morgan State College (B)	1867	State funded: undergraduate, graduate, evening programs	308	4,971 undergraduate 749 graduate
University of Maryland Baltimore (W)	1963	State funded: undergraduate,	283	4,353[a]
Greensboro, North Carolina North Carolina Agricultural and Technical State University (B)	1891	State funded: undergraduate, graduate programs	300	4,119 undergraduate 391 graduate
University of North Carolina, Greensboro (W)	1891	State funded: undergraduate, graduate programs	622	6,687 undergraduate 2,722 graduate
Montgomery, Alabama Alabama State University (B)	1866	State funded: undergraduate, graduate, evening programs	233	3,600 + (approx.)
Auburn University (W)	1967	State funded: undergraduate, graduate, evening programs	204	3,547 undergraduate 250 graduate
Nashville, Tennessee Tennessee State University (B)	1912	State funded: undergraduate, graduate, evening programs	326	5,542[a]
University of Tennessee Nashville (W)	1947	State funded: evening, graduate, and MBA programs	328	5,600[a]
Savannah, Georgia Savannah State College (B)	1890	State funded: undergraduate; joint graduate programs with Armstrong	136	2,508[a] undergraduate and graduate
Armstrong State College (W)	1935	State funded: undergraduate; joint graduate programs with Savannah State	168	3,700 undergraduate and graduate

[a] 1978 Information Please Almanac.

cultural and Technical State University, was founded in the same year as the University of North Carolina at Greensboro. The mean age of the black colleges is 92.8 years, compared to 37.4 years for the white colleges. This fact indicates that the black colleges have an older heritage and educational tradition to offer the students than do the white colleges.

A charge often leveled at black colleges is that they are ingrown, that is, that a high proportion of their faculties graduated from the schools in which they now teach. The assumption is that institutional inbreeding is unhealthy. We found that 28.5 percent of the faculty members at predominantly black schools in this study compared with 13.6 percent of the faculty members in the predominantly white schools were alumni of the institutions in which they taught.

However, at both types of schools, more than two-thirds of the faculty members received all their degrees at colleges and universities other than those of current employment. This fact disproves the charge that either black or white public colleges are ingrown. This finding may forestall further efforts by some educators to explain the beneficial or negative effects of academic inbreeding in black public institutions of higher education as if this practice were an established fact.

To study further the extent of the diversification of predominantly black compared with predominantly white public college faculties, we examined these questions: Which faculty is more cosmopolitan? What has been the interracial, interregional, and international formal educational experience of the teaching faculty?

Faculties of the predominantly black public colleges in this study are indeed different from those of the predominantly white schools (table 10-2). Only 2 percent of the faculty members at predominantly white colleges had received an academic degree from a predominantly black public or private college. Of the faculty at predominantly white schools, 3.8 percent had academic degrees from foreign colleges and universities. The overwhelming experience of the white faculty at predominantly white public colleges was an intraracial experience in formal education; 94 percent of the faculty

Table 10-2
Type of Institutions from Which Faculty Members Received Degrees

	Black Colleges Only		Black and White Colleges		White Colleges Only		Foreign Institutions		
	N	%	N	%	N	%	N	%	Total
Black colleges	273	21.0	578	44.4	344	26.9	108	8.3	1,303
White colleges	11	0.7	31	2.0	1,502	93.6	61	3.8	1,605

members at predominantly white colleges in this study obtained their academic education from predominantly white schools. In contrast, 26.9 percent of the faculty at predominantly black schools had been educated at predominantly white schools only; 21 percent had attended black schools only. A majority had received academic degrees from both black and white schools and from foreign institutions. The 8.3 percent of faculty members in predominantly black public colleges that graduated from foreign colleges or universities was twice the proportion of faculty in predominantly white schools that had this experience.

The interregional educational experiences of the faculties of the predominantly black and the predominanlty white institutions are illustrated by comparing the two schools in Nashville, Tennessee. The catalogue for Tennessee State University (TSU), the predominantly black school, reveals a faculty with a rich mixture of formal education in eastern, midwestern, and southern public and private institutions. Nearly half of that faculty (49.4 percent) received their highest degrees from institutions located outside the South compared to only 27.7 percent of the faculty at the predominantly white University of Tennessee at Nashville. Nearly half of the faculty members at the predominantly white institution received their highest degrees within the state of Tennessee, compared to 37.7 percent of the faculty at TSU.

Based on the analysis of these data, we conclude that the teaching faculties of predominantly black public colleges and universities are much more cosmopolitan than their counterparts in predominantly white institutions. This study found the faculties of predominantly black public colleges and universities to be a rich composite of interracial, interregional, and international experiences in formal education. These data support Tobe Johnson's contention that "the black college faculties are the only faculties in the country which are multiracial and multiethnic in more than a token sense" (1971, p. 805).

The characteristics of the faculties examined thus far differ from those usually considered in assessing instructional quality. Nevertheless, they are important. The diversity of experience and the cosmopolitan character of a faculty are as significant as enhancements to the instructional role as the level or depth of education that members have received.

We turn now to an analysis of the level of education of the faculties of the predominantly black and predominantly white public colleges in this study to determine differences, if any, in amount of formal training. Traditionally, this characteristic of the faculty has been given more attention in assessment of quality. Table 10-3 reveals that 56.8 percent of the faculty in the predominantly white publicly supported colleges compared with 41.4 percent of the faculty in similar predominantly black schools had earned doctoral degrees. At the same time, proportionately fewer persons with

Table 10-3

Highest Degree Level of Faculty Members at Predominantly Black Colleges and Predominantly White Colleges

| | Highest Degree Level Reached | | | | | | |
| | Bachelor's | | Master's | | Doctor's | | |
	N	%	N	%	N	%	Total
Black colleges	64	4.9	699	53.6	540	41.4	1,303
White colleges	116	7.2	578	36.0	911	56.8	1,605

only a bachelor's degree were accepted as bonafide faculty members at the predominantly black school (4.9 percent) compared with the predominantly white (7.9 percent) school.

Aggregated data, however, can be misleading. To determine variations masked by the summary figures, we analyzed the faculties of predominantly black and predominantly white public institutions by highest academic degree achieved for each of the five cities. The data are presented in table 10-4. In Maryland, for example, we found great variation, with the proportion of faculty in the predominantly white school in Baltimore having twice as many faculty members with the doctoral degree as its predominantly black counterpart. In Savannah, Georgia, we found the opposite, but to a lesser extent. The faculty with the higher proportion of members with doctoral degrees was the predominantly white institution in which the number of doctorates was 45.2 percent. In Montgomery, Alabama, the predominantly black and predominantly white schools were almost identical (47.2 percent and 48 percent, respectively) in the proportion of their faculties with doctoral degrees. These data indicate that one should not assume that all black schools are similar in the quality of their faculties, just as all white schools are not similar.

Despite the fact that, in general, public white colleges in this study tended to employ as faculty members a higher proportion of scholars who had earned a doctoral degree, it should be noted that a substantial number of faculty members at both predominantly black and predominantly white public colleges that have campuses in the same city are without the doctoral degree. Slightly less than five out of every ten faculty members at predominantly white schools, and almost six out of every ten faculty members at predominantly black schools in this study, had not received the highest academic degree. This fact alone suggests that the faculties probably could be strengthened if resources were concentrated on staffing one rather than two institutions. We conclude that neither the black nor the white public colleges have strong faculties in terms of highest degree achieved.

A range of characteristics should be considered in any proposal for consolidating black and white schools. The faculty's cosmopolitan experience

Table 10-4
Highest Degree Level of Faculty Members by City

	Bachelor's		Master's		Doctor's		
	N	%	N	%	N	%	Total
Baltimore							
Morgan State College (B)	21	6.8	169	54.9	118	38.3	308
University of Maryland (W)	15	5.3	45	15.9	223	78.8	283
Greensboro							
North Carolina Agricultural and Technical State University (B)	15	5.7	116	55.3	117	39.0	300
University of North Carolina, Greensboro (W)	35	5.6	219	35.2	368	59.2	622
Montgomery							
Alabama State University (B)	7	3.0	116	48.8	110	47.2	233
Auburn University (W)	14	6.9	92	45.1	98	48.0	204
Nashville							
Tennessee State University (B)	12	3.7	192	58.9	112	37.4	326
University of Tennessee, Nashville (W)	37	11.3	195	44.2	146	44.5	328
Savannah							
Savannah State College (B)	7	5.1	56	41.2	73	53.7	136
Armstrong State College (W)	15	8.9	77	45.8	76	45.2	168

as well as level of academic achievement should be analyzed in any policy decisions pertaining to desegregating predominantly black and predominantly white institutions of higher education and creating a unitary system of publicly supported instruction for higher education. This analysis reveals that predominantly black and predominantly white public institutions have assets and liabilities. The predominantly white institution, in instances in which two public schools are in the same city, tends to have the more qualified faculty in terms of cosmopolitan experience—interracial, interregional, and international. Each of these two different qualities is significant. They are trade-off characteristics in any equation of the quality of faculty. Predominantly black and predominantly white faculties in public colleges and institutions that are located in the same city tend to be more dissimilar in their cosmopolitan characteristics than in their academic levels of achievements, as represented by highest degree received.

Conclusion

On the basis of the analysis presented in this chapter, we recommend that the following three characteristics be examined in order to determine which institution is to be maintained as a way of merging two previously segregated colleges: first, intangible educational qualities such as the length of time campuses have been in existence and concomitant values associated with educational practices that have evolved over the years; second, the physical plant and setting of the institutions; and third, the characteristics of faculties, including academic preparation and cosmopolitan experiences.

A previous study of desegregation at the elementary school level provides support for the assumption that cosmpolitan characteristics of faculty members facilitate a smooth desegregation process. A comparison of a school that catered to a more or less homogeneous middle-class white population and had an excellent academic reputation with a school with a good academic rating as well as the capacity to teach physically handicapped children indicated that the latter school went through a smoother desegregation process than the former. The ability of the faculty of the latter school to deal with a diverse group of students enabled them to cope effectively with a student body whose racial composition changed as a result of a desegregation plan. The authors of this study state that "the findings . . . suggest that an educational environment . . . that fosters the integration and assimilation of all sorts and conditions of people, including all races and social classes, must include an orientation among teachers and administrators of accepting persons as they are, as well as an orientation toward achievement and high aspirations" (Willie and Beker 1973, p. 45).

The cosmopolitan experiences of predominantly black college faculties have enabled them to develop a "double consciousness" that has sensitized them to the needs of others as well as to their own interests. They have developed this characteristic because it is one of the goals of education in black colleges. Another goal of predominantly black colleges has been that of seeking a "double victory" in which the former oppressed and the former oppressors are mutually fulfilled (Willie and Hedgepeth 1978). This orientation, which was discussed in detail in chapter 1, should enable predominantly black schools, such as Tennessee State University, to adapt to their new status as the home campus for a racially integrated student body in a way that is fair to all.

These goals, of course, are not limited to predominantly black schools. They rightfully are goals for higher education universally but have been nurtured and kept alive in the United States by predominantly black public and private institutions. If predominantly white or black colleges are to desegregate and integrate, in instances in which one is proposed as the surviving institution for a unitary system, these are the terms under which such action should proceed.

References

Adams v. *Richardson* 1974. 480 F. 2d 1159. Now *Adams* v. *Weinberger.*

Browning, Jane Smith. 1975. "The Origins, Development, and Desegregation of the Traditionally Black Public Colleges and Universities, 1837-1975." Cambridge: Harvard Graduate School of Education dissertation.

Jencks, Christopher, and Riesman, David. 1967. "The American Negro College." *Harvard Educational Review* 37(Winter):3-60.

Johnson, Tobe. 1971. "The Black College System." *Daedalus* 100:798-812.

Pressley, Sam W. 1978. "Changing Times at Cheyney." Philadelphia: *The Sunday Bulletin Discoverer* (February 28):6-7, 19.

Smith, Charles U. 1978. "Teaching and Learning the Social Sciences in the Predominantly Black Universities." In *Black Colleges in America,* edited by Charles V. Willie and R.E. Edmonds. New York: Teachers College Press.

Thompson, Daniel C. 1973. *Private Black Colleges at the Crossroads.* Westport, Conn.: Greenwood Press.

U.S. Bureau of the Census. 1975. *The Social and Economic Status of the Black Population in the United States 1974.* Washington, D.C.: U.S. Government Printing Office.

_____. 1977. *Statistical Abstract of the United States.* Washington, D.C.: U.S. Government Printing Office.

Willie, Charles V., and Beker, J. 1973. *Race Mixing in the Public Schools.* New York: Praeger.

Willie, Charles V., and Hedgepeth, Chester. 1978. "The Goals of Black Colleges." *Journal of Higher Education:*89-96.

Willie, Charles V., and MacLeish, Marlene Y. 1976. "Priorities of Black College Presidents." *Educational Record* 57 (Spring):92-100.

11 The Function and Future of Black Colleges and Universities

The issues with which black colleges and universities are wrestling today are those that bear directly on the future of all higher education in this nation. One could call black educational institutions the research and development arm of higher education. These institutions have experimented with ways of effectively involving students in governance and in relevant community services. They were among the first to implement open-admissions policies. They demonstrated that classical and career educations can be united within a single curriculum. They established informal faculty tutors for promising students. These and other innovations now have been adopted by other colleges and universities.

The minority is a curious reflection of the majority. I say curious because in the human social system, the minority provides a double reflection. It indicates what the society has been and what it can be. Richard Wright recognized this fact several decades ago when he wrote, "We black folk, our history and our present being, are a mirror of all the manifold experiences of America."

Wright said that American whites can understand themselves as the majority better by looking at and coming to know the minority. In a poetic phrase, he said, *"We* are *you* looking back at you from the dark mirror of our lives." Then he said, "What we want, what we represent, what we endure is what America *is*" (Wright and Rosskam 1941, pp. 145-146). This idea is not different from that expressed by Eric Hoffer, a former laborer on the waterfront, when he described the middle classes as "the inert mass of a nation" that is "worked upon and shaped by minorities" (Hoffer 1963, p. 148). These ideas are different from those advanced by public officials such as Daniel Patrick Moynihan, who suggested that the progress of the minority is seriously retarded when its way of life "is out of line with the rest of American society" (U.S. Department of Labor 1965, p. 29). The Moynihan frame of reference suggests that minorities should be essentially other-directed and imitative. Using a similar frame of reference, Christopher Jencks and David Riesman (1967, p. 21) characterized black colleges of the mid-twentieth century as "an ill-financed, ill-staffed caricature of white higher education."

Ernest Holsendolph, writing in a 1971 issue of *Fortune* magazine, said that "the lowering of racial barriers in the United States during the past two decades . . . has clouded the future of the institutions that up to now have borne much of the burden of educating the teachers, lawyers, ministers, and other leaders of black America'' (1971, p. 104). Among the questions raised by public policymakers and educators, according to Holsendolph, are these: Should there be black colleges at all? Should society perpetuate black colleges when white schools are opening to black students and in some cases actively recruiting them? Has history bypassed black colleges? .

To attempt to answer these questions about the future of black colleges and universities without first pondering their function can lead to inappropriate conclusions and a disastrous national policy with reference to higher education. Benjamin E. Mays asked the rhetorical question: "Why pick out Negro colleges and say they must die?" Then he said, "If America allows black colleges to die, it will be the worst kind of discrimination and denigration known in history." If these colleges are blotted out, Mays told the Black College Conference at Harvard in 1976, "You blot out the image of black men and women in education" (1978, pp. 19-28). If the image of the minority is blotted out of education, the majority, according to Wright, cannot know itself.

Not all agree with this conclusion. Both blacks and whites, inside and outside the civil rights movement, have been critical of the continued existence of black colleges. These critical statements usually focus on whether there should be a future for black colleges, and they usually give inadequate attention to the function of these colleges. The critics reveal the superficiality of their analysis by their silence on whether higher education in America would have a future without black colleges.

It is difficult for predominantly black schools to get a hearing regarding what they can, could, and should do not only for blacks but for the education of the nation. Failure to learn from the innovative pedagogical methods and techniques that have emerged over the years from the black experience in America could be a hinderance to future developments in higher education for the majority as well as the minority population. The approach of the minority may in the end be of value to the majority as stated earlier by Wright and Hoffer.

Moral and Ethical Issues

To put it bluntly, black colleges and universities have kept alive interest in the pursuit of honesty, justice, and altruism or sacrifice as goals of higher education. They have helped the nation recognize a range of desirable characteristics in students and the difference between information and knowledge, on the one hand, and virtue and wisdom, on the other, and how these complement each other. Two of America's foremost educators declared that "the best single measure over-all" of academic competence is the "verbal aptitude test" (Jencks and Riesman 1967, p. 476). Clearly our definition of academic competence is too narrow if it is limited to the development of verbal skills. Most teachers in predominantly black colleges believe that developing moral and ethical competency is desirable too. The data presented in chapter 5 indicate that this definition of desirability also is shared by white college teachers. Black colleges and universities have brought these characteristics to the attention of the public through the behavior of their students and graduates. The sit-ins, freedom rides, and civil rights' demonstrations were led by black college students and black college graduates who rescued the nation from the scourge of segregation.

During the closing years of the 1970s the leaders of academic institutions across the nation wrestled with the moral and ethical issues that involve their schools as responsible investors in corporations that transact business in South Africa. After a great deal of soul searching, Derek Bok, the president of Harvard came forth with a question and an affirmation. This information is reported here so that it may be compared with the philosophy of a leader of a black college several years earlier. The president of Harvard said this: "Injustice and suffering are plainly matters of grave concern. . . . We may expect the University not to act deliberately to increase the suffering of others. But the principal issue before us is whether we should go further and use the University as a means of expressing moral disapproval or as a weapon in our fight against injustice even if we threaten to injure the academic functions of the institution." This was his unanswered question.

The assertion by the Harvard president, however, indicated the answer toward which he was leaning. He said, "Universities are designed to achieve particular purposes. Their special mission is the discovery and transmission of knowledge. . . . [Their] *institutional* goal is not to reform society in specific ways. Universities have neither the mandate nor the competence to administer foreign policy, set our social and economic priorities, enforce standards of conduct in the society, or carry out other social functions apart from learning and discovery." Moreover, the Harvard president asserted, "We should also recognize that very rarely will the institutional acts of a single university—or even universities as a group—have any substantial possibility of putting an end to the misfortunes that exist in society" (Bok 1979).

Back in 1945, when Martin Luther King, Jr. was completing his freshman year at Morehouse College, the president of that school said in a radio address: "It will not be sufficient for Morehouse College . . . to produce clever graduates, men fluent in speech and able to argue their way through; but rather honest men, men who are sensitive to the wrongs, the sufferings, and the injustices of society and who are willing to accept responsibility for correcting the ills" (quoted in Bennet 1977, p. 78). In this passage, spoken more than two decades before the death of one of the college's most famous graduates, Martin Luther King, Jr., this black college administrator established a set of priorities in which honesty, a cultivated characteristic, is more valued than verbal facility. Ten years later in the Montgomery bus boycott of 1955-1956, Martin Luther King, Jr. acted out the words of his college president. Through his courageous civil rights' campaigns, King went on to become, in the words of Charles Merrill, "the closest this country has to a saint" (1978, p. 170). Note that the predominantly white college president emphasized analysis and the predominantly black college president emphasized analysis and action. Moreover, the predominantly black college administrator emphasized action as a moral responsibility of the educated person. Further discussion of the moral responsibility of educational institutions will be presented in chapter 15.

Historian L.D. Reddick described the black college that King experienced as a place where "teachers encouraged their students to explore and search for solutions to campus and world problems," a place where "nobody on the faculty seemed to be afraid to think and speak out," a place where the president "was willing to be counted" (1959, p. 70). King's dedication to social justice apparently was related to his Morehouse College education.

King's black college president not only offered useful ideas but also support in time of trouble. In his autobiography, *Born to Rebel,* Benjamin Mays tells us of a meeting that he attended that was arranged by the father of Martin Luther King, Jr.:

> When the Montgomery officials discovered that violence could not stay the protest or stop the [bus] boycott, they resorted to mass arrest. . . . Dr. King was in Nashville, . . . at that time [he] knew that if he returned to Montgomery he would be arrested too. Enroute to Montgomery he stopped overnight in Atlanta. His father, frantic for his son's safety, assembled a group of [eight] friends to consult with them about the wisdom of Martin Luther, Jr.'s immediate return to Montgomery. . . . Reverend King, Sr. stated his reason for calling [the group] together and expressed his conviction that his son should not return to Montgomery right away (Mays 1969, p. 267).

In *Stride Toward Freedom,* his account of the Montgomery bus boycott, Martin Luther King, Jr. described what went on in that meeting. He said that he listened to these men because they were his elders and their word commanded respect. After hearing them out, he told the small group of elders that it would be the height of cowardice to stay away from Montgomery when his friends and associates were being arrested, that he had begun the struggle and could not turn back, that he had reached the point of no return. After his response, silence fell upon the room, and his father began to cry. At this point, Benjamin Mays, his former college president, began to defend him and defended young Martin's position strongly (King 1958).

Later Mays said, "I had to defend Martin Luther [King, Jr.'s] position. Here was a man of deep integrity and firm conviction. How could he have decided otherwise than to return to Montgomery?" Mays also said that he was glad that he had the wisdom to give his former student the moral support that was needed at that time. Mays concluded his report of that episode with a statement of admiration for Martin Luther King, Jr.: "I had admired him ever since he entered Morehouse as a freshman; now my respect for him mounted on wings" (Mays 1969, p. 268).

At Morehouse, a predominantly black college, freedom and equality were valued. At Morehouse King was taught that justice had to be sought and could not be taken for granted. At Morehouse he was told about his responsibility to help the poor, oppressed, and afflicted. At Morehouse King received a black college education from which the whole nation has benefited.

What Morehouse College did for Martin Luther King, Jr. is similar to what other black colleges have done for their graduates. Gregory Kannerstein, who has studied the self-concept of several black colleges, concluded that "perhaps the greatest and most distinctive contribution of black colleges to the American philosophy of higher education has been to emphasize and legitimate public and community service as a major objective of colleges and universities." Kannerstein said statements of the purpose of most black colleges reveal a "litany of 'education-citizenship-leadership-democracy' that affirms a belief in the democratic process and in the ability of colleges, students, and alumni to influence it" (1978, pp. 31, 39).

Even though the black college that Martin Luther King, Jr. attended emphasized service and citizenship, it also provided him with a good education that developed other academic skills. In fact, one-tenth of its graduates have earned an academic or professional doctoral degree. Thus, a focus on service and citizenship need not result in neglect of the cultivation of other capacities. Most black colleges have provided their students with a comprehensive education that focused on purpose as well as method. Predominantly black Howard University, for example, is probably the most integrated educational institution in the United States. Receiving an education in an integrated setting is a distinct educational asset for people who live in a pluralistic and cosmopolitan society. The future of black colleges, therefore, is assured if the nation fully understands their function—that of fulfilling the values of the society at large sometimes better than institutions that are controlled by members of the majority.

Integration

One value of the society at large fulfilled by black colleges better than any other educational institutions is that of integrating the races. Black colleges have demonstrated how to do this from their beginning. The Office for Advancement of Public Negro Colleges of the National Association of State Universities and Land-Grant Colleges (1978) reported in the August *Advancement Newsletter* that "approximately fifteen percent (15%) of the total number of students graduating from historically black public colleges are classified as nonblack." Few predominantly white colleges have desegregated to the extent that one-sixth of their graduates are black. Black colleges have been segregated by law, but they never have been segregating institutions. Many were founded with racially integrated faculties. They could teach other institutions how to become pluralistic in a desegregating society.

If the state plans for implementing the *Adams* v. *Richardson* decision consider this goal of higher education that predominantly black institutions have fulfilled—that of bringing their students and faculty into contact with racial groups other than their own—then the identity of predominantly black colleges will be preserved. For there will be no need to dissolve predominantly black schools to achieve the goal of diversity.

Alternative Plans for Desegregation

The future for black institutions of higher education will depend on whether they seize the planning opportunities presented by the *Adams* case and propose alternative arrangements that perpetuate predominantly black colleges and universities. Harold Howe II, former commissioner of education of the United States, said, "The federal government should not be in the business of deciding which institutions should survive and which should not, although it should offer a powerful supportive hand to the traditionally black colleges that have suffered both discrimination and neglect in America for many years" (1979).

Whites ought to know as much about honesty, justice, and altruism or sacrifice as blacks. They can learn these things that they ought to know by experiencing the status of a minority. Whites can serve in the status of a racial minority in America only if there are predominantly black or predominantly brown colleges, universities, and other institutions in which to participate, as mentioned in several other chapters in this book, particularly chapter 3. Thus, the retention of predominantly black colleges and universities in the United States is for the benefit of whites as well as of blacks.

In a report to the annual meeting of the Associated Harvard Alumni, President Derek Bok said, "It would be folly to assume that the government will not continue to intervene, or to content ourselves with last-minute efforts to block legislation and preserve the status quo." Bok called upon colleges and universities to seize the initiative and help to devise new mechanisms that will enable higher education to work with the government to ensure that universities respond to public needs without being subject to restrictions that ignore their ability to be of continuing use to society (Willie 1978, p. 170). It is time for black colleges and universities to seize this initiative and develop alternative plans for the desegregation of higher education. In the past, blacks seized the initiative in Reconstruction state legislatures and developed plans to enrich the nation through state-supervised local systems of public education.

The record is in favor of rather than against the continued existence of predominantly black colleges. A self-centered attempt, however, to save black colleges and universities for blacks will be as damaging as an other-directed recommendation to remake these institutions in the image of white ones. Both actions ultimately will end in defeat. Black colleges and universities must be saved for the value they add to the society for all in demonstrating how to achieve a double victory for the former oppressed and the former oppressors. Black colleges and universities have a future in our society because of their function in it.

I conclude this chapter by returning to the wisdom of Richard Wright and Eric Hoffer. There is an earthy quality about both men. Wright characterized America's largest racial minority as "the dark mirror" that reflects the lives of whites in such a way that they can see and know themselves better. Hoffer called the subdominant people of power "the dregs" who, as they rise to the top, manifest the innermost worth of a nation. In the system of higher education in the United States, black colleges and universities are analogous to "the dark mirror" because they have been ignored as if they were invisible, and to "the dregs" because they have been put down and collectively called "an academic disaster area."

If Wright and Hoffer are correct, it would be a disaster to dismantle black colleges and universities, for whites would be destroying the best reflection available of the state of their own manners and morals and the innermost worth of higher education. In this new age of desegregation and integration, the value of an institution will be determined not by how well it treats the majority but by how merciful it is to the minority. In this respect, black colleges and universities can serve as a model for many by demonstrating that the way to educational enhancement for a black majority is through compassion and concern for a white minority.

References

Bennett, L. 1977. "The Last of the Great Schoolmasters." *Ebony,* December, p. 78.

Bok, D.C. 1979. "Supplement to the Harvard University *Gazette,*" 9 March.

Hoffer, Eric. 1963. *The Ordeal of Change.* New York: Harper & Row.

Holsendolph, Ernest. 1971. "Black Colleges Are Worth Saving." *Fortune* October, pp. 104-122.

Howe, Harold II. 1979. "Colleges in the 1980s." Speech delivered at Salem Academy and College, February.

Jencks, Christopher, and Riesman, David. 1967. "The American Negro College." *Harvard Educational Review* 37 (Summer).

Kannerstein, Gregory. 1978. "Black Colleges: Self-Concept." In *Black Colleges in America,* edited by Charles V. Willie and R.E. Edmonds. New York: Teachers College Press.

King, Martin Luther, Jr. 1958. *Stride Toward Freedom: The Montgomery Story.* New York: Harper & Row.

Mays, Benjamin E. 1969. *Born to Rebel.* New York: Scribner's.

———. 1978. "Black Colleges in Higher Education." In *Black Colleges in America,* edited by Charles V. Willie and R.E. Edmonds. New York: Teachers College Press.

Merrill, C. 1978. "The Board of Trustees and the Black College." In *Black Colleges in America*, edited by Charles V. Willie and R.E. Edmonds. New York: Teachers College Press.

Office for Advancement of Public Negro Colleges of the National Association of State Universities and Land-Grant Colleges. 1978. *Advancement Newsletter* (August).

Reddick, L.D. 1959. *Crusader Without Violence.* New York: Harper & Row

U.S. Department of Labor. 1965. *The Negro Family.* Washington, D.C.: U.S. Government Printing Office.

Willie, Charles V. 1978. *The Sociology of Urban Education.* Lexington, Mass. Lexington Books, D.C. Heath and Co.

Wright, R., and Rosskam, E. 1941. *12 Million Black Voices.* New York: Viking.

**Part V
The Curriculum and
Educational Materials**

12 Black Studies

Blacks insist on the immediate application of knowledge to the solution of community problems. They believe that a black studies program will accommodate this interest, that it will be less theoretical and more pragmatic, and that it will deal with real and relevant issues. A few black students perceive the black studies program as a protective suit of armor, insulating them from a hostile white educational environment. They are fearful of being whitewashed in other courses designed and taught by whites.

Working with people rather than with things is important to black students. Of black students studied at four upstate New York colleges, 70 to 75 percent indicated that they are oriented to occupations that involve working with people. (A majority of white students have a similar orientation. However, only 55 to 60 percent of all white students, compared with the 70-75 percent of blacks, feel this is a very important goal of a college education.) This is reflected in their choice of majors. For example, at Cosmopolitan College, the highest proportion of black students, 39 percent, were majoring in the social and behavioral sciences, with psychology, sociology, and political science the most popular majors. One-third of the blacks are in professional programs, particularly education and business administration. The remainder, 27 percent, was equally divided between the humanities, the physical and biological sciences, and mathematics.

Although psychology, sociology, political science, education, and business administration are considered by many blacks to be more relevant than other fields of study, some students assert that the ideas and information presented in all courses are useless and will be useless to them after graduation. This is the opinion of 55 percent of the black students included in our study. Blacks expect the social and behavioral sciences to deal with "real problems." In general, course content is described as real or relevant if it focuses upon the black experience. Some black students speak disparagingly of art courses that are concerned with the ancient Greeks and Romans. Others are uninterested in international relations. Courses that impart information about American historical heroes such as George Washington are described by some blacks as "brainwashing experiences."

Reprinted with permission from *Black Students at White Colleges*, by Charles V. Willie and Arline McCord, New York: Praeger Special Studies Series, 1972, chapter 4. Slightly revised.

Many blacks maintain that college courses ignore black problems and black life styles. There are, for example, many complaints that black authors and black poets are ignored. Because black literature is seldom assigned, black students feel that they do not get an opportunity to learn things about themselves. Consequently, they believe that "black students don't learn much that would add . . . to their abilities." John, a second-year student who was born in a large city ghetto, described the need of black students to learn more about their people as "a necessary thing." Music at his school was offered as one example of the avoidance of black life styles. Some black students were critical of the lack of emphasis on jazz in music courses. They considered jazz to be a unique expression of the black experience and were disappointed that formal instruction in this music form was not available at most white colleges.

Students enrolled in courses in methods of education have had difficulty in securing experience as practice teachers in ghetto schools. Most arrangements for supervised classroom teaching at elementary and secondary school levels are made with affluent suburban school systems. Few blacks live in the communities surrounding these schools. For these and other reasons, the black students conclude that the education they are getting is geared toward whites and that their professors do not appreciate the black experience.

Black students accept the fact that some black people need to be trained as physicians, lawyers, and scientists. They do not set forth a program in black studies as a substitute for these disciplines. However, the process of labeling courses as "white-oriented" and the press for black awareness may create some identity conflicts for black students pursuing study in the sciences or professions. In a rap session on one campus, the black students said that black professionals play an important part in strengthening the black community. These students saw the black studies program as a way of equipping the professionals with a state of mind that would enable them to go back into the community to serve the people. Blacks also believe that they ought to have the privilege of majoring in black studies if they wish to do so.

Black students want black studies to fulfill a multitude of purposes. This may constitute the major difficulty in instituting such a program. It is proposed as a means of learning essential information, understanding the history of one's people, promoting black identity and solidarity, providing relevant academic experiences, straightening out oneself, and charting goals for the future. Thus, the program is expected to deal with the present as well as the past, and with personal as well as public concerns. It should convey a body of information, as well as induce a certain outlook on life or state of mind. It is fair to say that black students expect black studies to deal with both the prophetic and the pragmatic. As stated by Jim: "We are working on a life-time thing. With the creation of a black studies program, I think we will have a black renaissance on a small scale right here. Creativity will bloom. Wow! Black studies will just make things blossom—for me, anyway, and I think I speak for a lot of my brothers and sisters.''

The black studies program also would meet the criterion of relevancy alluded to so frequently by the black students. Relevancy is defined succinctly by Bill as "anything which has to do with me." Black students believe that anything having to do with their way of life is ignored or rejected by white teachers. Mary, a freshman, said that "the black studies program being pushed by the Black Student Union is one of the best things." She talks about the black studies course in music literature at her school and describes it as "a comfortable atmosphere where you're learning about something you want to learn." This student also likes her English class, because the professor uses a lot of "black books." Several students, particularly those who have grown up in big northern cities, state that they are bothered because they do not know much about their backgrounds. The future, the present, and the past are united in the minds of many black students. They believe that knowledge about the past is an important prelude for the future. This statement is representative of the ideas of many: "We're going to have to know more about our history to know who we are and where we are going."

A few blacks want a black studies program because it will benefit the whole school, including the white students. They see such a program providing much needed information for whites. One student concludes that whites have cheated themselves educationally for hundreds of years because of the exclusion of information about blacks. Mike summarized his thoughts in this short phrase: "Whites need to learn about us." Another student thought that whites not only would learn about blacks but eventually would adopt a black perspective by being exposed to black studies. "With the initiation of our methods in the whole aspect of college life, the white school will learn from it," said Clarence. He continued, "I believe, just like the white man steals anything hip in our culture like music and dances, he will steal our educational methods; he will steal our outlook on life." Another student, Bob, speaks of the contribution that a black studies program could make to the entire school, but he is quick to point out that the program first must consider the needs of blacks and that the contribution must be made on the terms of blacks: "Ultimately, the black studies program is for all kinds of students, but it should be geared toward the blacks."

There is almost universal agreement among black students that there should be a program of black studies at white colleges, and they also believe that the program should be controlled by blacks. There is disagreement among blacks as to whether the program should be available to whites. When black studies is looked upon as a way of teaching whites about blacks, the black students tend to be against establishing a separate program. When the primary purpose is to help blacks learn about themselves, and the teaching of whites is secondary, then black students tend to prefer and even lobby for a separate degree-granting program.

Most blacks included in this study, and particularly blacks from stable working-class and middle-class families, preferred a black studies program with a sufficient number of courses to permit a major or minor concentration. The few blacks who did not push for a separate program feel that such a program might attract only a few whites and that most white students would continue to take the traditional courses in which the black experience is omitted, ignored, or distorted and would thus remain ignorant. These few blacks thought that initially effort should be devoted.to getting all courses revised so that whites who are not likely to enroll in courses in a separate black studies program could learn why blacks are not going to take any more of the "mess" they have put up with in the past. Even blacks who are interested in a separate black studies program share the view that existing courses throughout the college need revising so that they incorporate more accurately the black experience in America. However, most blacks see this as a major effort, involving a great hassle with a doubtful outcome.

Apparently, the majority of black students have given up on attempts to educate whites by friendly persuasion. With the growing interest in awareness and self-knowledge, they are more concerned with developing separate academic structures where blacks can "do their own thing." Moreover, they look upon a degree-granting Department of Black Studies as a power base in the academic community, from which they can negotiate with strength. With a separate department, it would be easier to get the courses and faculty they desire.

Both political power interests and academic concerns are joined in proposals for black studies. For this reason, most black students no longer care to cajole or persuade whites to include appropriate materials about blacks in white-controlled courses. They have turned their attenton to educating themselves in a structure over which they have some control. The overwhelming call for a separate black studies department is best understood as a manifestation of the growing movement for self-determination. Thus, the decision of whether or not to establish a black studies department no longer can be limited to only subject-matter considerations.

Black students believe that courses in black studies ought to be taught by black professors, although they will accept a few white teachers if they clearly are a minority of the teaching faculty in the program. However, blacks stipulate that the few white instructors in black studies programs must be "extra qualified." The following black students discuss their preference for black or white teachers in black studies programs. These preferences are presented because they are typical of the responses of other blacks when asked to comment upon racial preference of teachers:

Ben: Only blacks should teach black studies courses because there are things one can't get out of books.

Jane: I would like to see a black person teaching the black studies course; but if there was a white person who was *exceptionally qualified*—but I would rather go out and look for a black person to fill the position first.

Sandra: I think that only blacks should teach these black studies courses because when you teach about black people, only blacks can relate their experiences to the person being taught.

Marsha: Black professors should be gotten to teach black courses whenever possible because with white profesors there would be a problem with communication. If a white professor is *extra qualified* to teach a black course, we should keep a close eye on him and be extra critical of what he is saying.

Louis: There should be an all-black or almost an all-black faculty in the black studies department.

Dennis: A black studies department should be established at this school and run by and for blacks. Power must be in the hands of the people who are directly concerned.

Allen: As far as faculty of the black studies program, I would say vie for all the black faculty you can; and then when you run out of qualified black people, go to *extra, extra qualified* whites.

Cheryl: Only black professors should teach these courses because they can relate to the course better: there's nothing like being black to deal with a black problem.

Black students insist that experience with blacks rather than knowledge of blacks is the important quality for teachers of black studies. Using experience as a major criterion, black students can rule out the employment of whites until available black teachers have been considered; few whites in this segregated society have participated meaningfully in the black experience. These students feel that no matter how concerned, sympathetic, and knowledgeable, whites must necessarily view the black experience from the outside. In this instance, intellectual and economic concerns are joined in the statement of the qualifications of teachers of black studies. By insisting that professors in black studies have authentic experiences in the black community, employment opportunities for the black studies faculty is limited largely to blacks.

These preferences also reveal important themes in the black experience. Apparently, blacks must accept a person first before they can accept his or her ideas. Race has long been an impediment to personal acceptance in American society, which is here manifested in the rejection of whites by blacks. Whites, whom blacks now personally reject, they also reject professionally. One should be reminded that the prejudicial attitudes of blacks toward whites revealed in this study are similar to the prejudicial attitude of whites toward blacks revealed in other studies. In fact, the often repeated statement that any white who teaches in a black studies program must be extra qualified is a duplication of the demand for superior black teachers by white colleges in the past.

Black studies is a bona fide academic program and deals with valid educational concerns. Black studies also is a political instrument through which power relationships between blacks and whites are balanced on white college campuses. Black studies is a means for employment for black professors at white institutions. Black studies is a manifestation of the movement for self-determination. Black studies is all of this—a complex and confounding program.

13 Group Names, Labels, and Stereotypes in Educational Materials

The Macmillan Publishing Company and its School Book Division have provided illustrative material for part of this discussion. Its Committee for Creating Positive Sexual and Racial Images in Educational Materials published guidelines for Macmillan authors, artists, and editors. The guidelines had a positive purpose—that of creating positive images. The publishing industry is in the business of communicating by way of language. Images are an important component in the anatomy of language. The committee members expressed the belief that the guidelines would "expand rather than restrict . . . opportunities to serve the needs of . . . readers" (Committee 1975, p. 2). In addition to this reason, the Committee listed two others for preparing the guidelines—one ethical and the other, economic. Ethical and economic concerns are not unrelated, as colleges and universities have discovered in their attempt to be responsible shareowners in corporations that transact business for profit in South Africa.

The committee said that textbook publishers have an ethical responsibility not to teach young girls or minority children that they are "second-class citizens." The committee acknowledged that textbooks have a "pervasive influence . . . on children's self-image" and that children, when they are taught mathematics and reading, "are also learning—sometimes subliminally—how society regards certain groups of people." The committee concluded that textbook publishers have what it characterized as "an awesome social responsibility" not to teach children "that one type of person has less value than another."

The committee confessed that the conscience of publishers about their social responsibility to create positive sexual and racial images for all has been "only recently recognized" (1975, p. 1). Having recognized this responsibility, the Macmillan Company decided to do something about it. To recognize that a practice is wrong and harmful to others and then not attempt to control the harmful effects when one has the authority and power to do so is immoral as well as unethical. A publishing company that recognizes that its textbooks have contained harmful material pertaining to women and racial minorities is committing an ethical act when it deliberately decides to change this oppressive practice.

Happily, Macmillan perceived a correlation between its ethical concern and its economic interest, which was another reason for issuing the guidelines. The Macmillan Committee discovered a trend among textbook adoption committees everywhere: "[they] are beginning to add sexism and racism criteria to their adoption requirements" (Committee 1975, p. 2). This action on the part of such textbook adoption committees is not entirely a function of a self-serving morality that members are imposing upon an innocent and unsuspecting society.

The Macmillan Company reported that women, alienated men, black people, American Indians, and the aged, among others, "are insisting upon positive changes" (Committee 1975, pp. 1-2). Books are published to be sold. If these categories of people identified are insisting on positive changes, it means that many in the American population are dissatisfied with the way in which they have been characterized in textbooks in the past. Apparently they do not like being depicted only as background figures, passive watchers from the sidelines, second-class citizens, or persons of less value than others. If textbook adoption committees are tending to adopt only those books that both acknowledge "the wide varied backgrounds and heritages of young readers" and recognize their "common human concerns, needs, and feelings that transcend these differences," then the publishers who insist on depicting the unique experiences of affluent, upper middle-class, white families only, ignoring the common concerns that they and others share, will be left behind in the competition for the sale of their products. It is a well-known fact that prejudice and discrimination tend to "bottom out" when they reduce the profit margin on the "bottom line." Out of such wisdom, solvency is maintained.

Clearly Macmillan was following a course of action that would fulfill its self-interest when the Committee for Creating Positive Sexual and Racial Images was formed and given the task of formulating guidelines for authors, designers, illustrators, and editors of textbooks.

Some did not see it that way. Writer James J. Kilpatrick, for example, delivered a broadside against the Macmillan Publishing Company. He called Macmillan's personnel "born-again egalitarians." He said that they had confessed their sins, repented, and embarked upon a new life. Moreover, he said that by today's egalitarian standards, "Macmillan has said and done the right thing" (Kilpatrick 1976, p. 85). These statements are all right at face value, but they really were intended as ridicule.

As Kilpatrick got more worked up over the guidelines, he denounced them as "a willful exercise in intellectual dishonesty." He accused the company of using its textbooks to "propagandize for a new social order" and implied that this was the purpose of the new guidelines (Kilpatrick 1976, p. 85). Susan Hernandez of the University of Indiana Press accused some people of propagandizing for the old social order (1976, p. 88). Kilpatrick probably could be included in such a list. He appeared to be propagandizing for the continuation of a social order which he understands, to which he has become accustomed, and that is controlled by people like him. Years ago

Robert Park said that "prejudice—that is, caste, class and race prejudice—in its more naive and innocent manifestations, is merely resistance of the social order to change" (quoted in Locke and Stern 1942, p. 246).

Kilpatrick admitted that "it is altogether desirable to abandon or to modify practices both cruel and stupid." But he sneered at the suggestion that a mother might be portrayed "working at her desk, while dad reads or clears the dining room table." He spoofs the suggestion in the guidelines that both sexes might be depicted as playing ball and that sometimes boys might be pictured as watching a girls' team play. He caps his analyses with a sarcastic conclusion that children would regard as fake an illustration of a "baseball team consisting of three white girls, two black girls, three white boys and a Chinese shortstop" (Kilpatrick 1976, p. 86). We hasten to add that this team was the product of Kilpatrick's imagination and not that of the Macmillan Committee.

Kilpatrick, of course, presented what he considered to be the most ludicrous textbook illustration imaginable to make his point that the Macmillan guidelines were ludicrous. And yet, by his imaginary illustration, he may have revealed how much he—a middle-class, middle-aged man—has been isolated physically and perceptually from the changing world about him. It is not ludicrous at all to encounter a collectivity similar to that which Kilpatrick imagined, perhaps not on a baseball field yet, but certainly elsewhere there are such collectivities. At Harvard, for example, where Cleveland Amory said, "In the old days students . . . were actually ranked . . . on the basis of their . . . families' social position" (Amory 1960, p. 264), and which always has had a plentiful supply of students from old New England families, I taught a seminar on race relations in education during the spring of 1976 that consisted of two black men, one black woman, one white Anglo-Saxon Protestant woman, two white Irish Catholic men, one Native American woman, and one Chinese-American man. Three years later, I team-taught a seminar on community decision-making and education that consisted of two Native American men, three Hispanic women (one Cuban, one Mexican-American, and one Puerto Rican), three blacks (one man and two women), and five whites (two Protestant men, one Roman Catholic man and woman, and one Jewish woman). It is not hard to imagine a gathering in America today that consists of the combination that Kilpatrick offered as a mockery.

Allen Grimshaw, former editor of *The American Sociologist*, was struck by the lack of agreement on appropriate remedies for achieving equality of opportunity in our society and devoted the May 1976 issue of that journal to a discussion of strategies for redress of discrimination. He reprinted Kilpatrick's commentary on the Macmillan guidelines and then invited seven people to respond. One response was from a person associated with a university press. Grimshaw said, "I find it interesting, incidentally, that we could find no representative of any commercial press willing to respond to Kilpatrick'' (1976, inside front cover). This information is not conveyed as a criticism of the commercial press; it is merely a report of the facts without interpretation. I was one of those asked to respond to Kilpatrick's commentary. My response was short and succinct:

> James Kilpatrick's comments on Macmillan's *Guidelines for Creating Positive Sexual and Racial Images in Educational Materials* distorts the substance of the document. To comment upon a distorted comment would compound the misinformation conveyed to the public. I therefore consulted the original document—a standard practice in scholarship—and found that it indeed is an honest, enlightened, and realistic policy that should be implemented not only by the ''authors, designers, illustrators, and editors of textbooks and classroom materials'' at Macmillan but by all.

> The *Guidelines* suggest that materials that are ''offensive or patronizing to women'' should not be published, that published materials should use ''a broad representation of black leaders and writers, both establishment-approved and controversial,'' and that Hispanic people should be shown in a variety of neighborhoods ''on all class levels.'' The purpose for doing this, according to Macmillan, is to give children an ''unbiased view of the full range of human potential,'' including the view that males may be *occasionally self-doubting, in need of reassurance and support* [emphasis mine].

> One might conjecture that Kilpatrick's sarcastic denunciation of these *Guidelines* for human decency probably reflect the unacknowledged self-doubt and insecurity of a man who fantasizes that men—and especially white men—ought to be always in charge and should be privileged to label others when they so choose.

> These Macmillan guidelines do not march to the drumbeat of any freedom movement. Macmillan, in business to sell books and classroom materials, has determined that ''textbook adoption committees everywhere are beginning to add sexism and racism criteria to their adoption requirements,'' and believes that these committees will recommend rejection of educational materials that stereotype women and minorities. Macmillan is wise to respond to a changing situation in which women and minorities have decided no longer to cooperate in their own oppression. This is the decision of women and minorities, not of Kilpatrick, and therefore will not be changed by his sarcasm. The *Guidelines* effectively answered Kilpatrick before he spoke; they state that ''the struggle to comprehend fully today's equality and liberation has been painful, for we must overcome fundamental premises on which our own lives were built—many of the premises we gleaned from the textbooks we used as children'' (Willie 1976, pp. 92-93).

And so it is with Kilpatrick and some others of his vintage. Their broadsides from an age gone by manifest the pain that adaptation to new circumstances and conditions engenders for those who wish to maintain the social order over which they rule or to which they have become accustomed. They should be granted no quarter to their quest to impose the practices of the past upon the present when such are obsolete and inappropriate in the light of new understandings. Their problem should be dealt with mercifully, and they should be accepted gracefully at the first sign of any inclination to become "born-again" people who believe in justice and equality for all.

Beyond fulfilling the requirements of justice, the use of literature and curriculum materials that reflect the range of human experience among the people of this and other nations is of extraordinary educational value. Reporting on the Native American experience, Ann Beuf said that "generalizations about 'Indians' necessarily distort the truth." Further, she said, "What Native Americans regarded as the wisdom of conservation and the co-existence of [people] and nature was regarded as ignorance and wastefulness by the white settlers" (Beuf 1977, pp. 16-17). It is perilous to continue to ignore the knowledge and wisdom of the universe and its people that have been discovered by various minority groups of our land.

An anthology on *Black Colleges in America* (Willie and Edmonds 1978) that indicated how these schools had done so much, so well, with so little was rejected by one university press. The manuscript was characterized as defective because there was "too much praise, and too much protest." To its credit, Teachers College Press of Columbia University published the book. Nancy Arnez has raised the critical question about an action such as that of the university press. "How can black people ignore these conditions of their lives and focus only on bees, birds, and trees?" She concludes that for some time to come, black writers must combine sociopolitical themes with the aesthetic (Arnez 1972, pp. 106-107).

Despite the style of presentation, there is much to learn from writers in racial and ethnic minority groups. Discussing the freshman English course at Miles College in Birmingham, Alabama, John Monro said, "Our reading is mostly from black authors . . . our students and faculty are deeply interested in developing a full and accurate awareness of the American black experience, historically, and its expression in literature." He criticized the public school system for not even trying to deal with the black experience. He saw his mission as providing the predominantly black student body at Miles with the basic information about the black experience that would "tell the truth [and] set . . . the record straight." He concluded that "the country would be much better off if white colleges would do the same" (Monro 1978, p. 245).

Words as Meaning-Carriers

If the issue were one only of style and manner, it would be less serious. We who make our living trafficking in words know that words have the specific role of being meaning-carriers. Clemens Benda, a psychiatrist with training also in philosophy, states that "the [human world] is not only interpreted and communicated through language but is experienced and evaluated through the meaningful framework provided by the language into which each individual is born" (1961, p. 95).

Benda continued his analysis of language and the anatomy of consciousness by discussing function and meaning. He said, "A concept never refers to an isolated form but to a function." To illustrate, chairs are something to sit on. "Thus any definition of chair which fails to take note of its function will be incomplete" (Benda 1961, p. 105). In a similar vein, James Greenough and George Kittredge, a classical philologist and an English literature scholar, stated that "words . . . have no character in themselves. They are merely conventional signs, and consequently they can be good or bad, dignified or vulgar, only in accordance with the ideas which they conventionally denote or suggest in the mind of the speaker and his [or her] hearers" (Greenough and Kittredge 1962, p. 224). A concrete example, according to Alain Locke and Bernard Stern, is the use of the "title, Mister." The title has no character of its own. In race relations, they said it symbolizes equality in the same way that denial of that title suggests social inequality in race and culture contact (Locke and Stern 1942, pp. 256-257).

Indeed, "the world of experience is given to [a child] as a world of named objects" (Benda 1961, p. 101). Thus, language, according to Benda, is "a means of influencing the inner world of the person" (1961, p. 107). If this is a true principle about the function of language, one can understand the contest among different groups to get their interpretation of reality accepted as the public interpretation of reality, as discussed in chapter 5. Such an interpretation has the power to influence the inner world of all people—those who are subdominant as well as those who are dominant in the power structure. Robert Merton has stated that the premise "that white (and for some, presumably only white) is true and good and beautiful" has been institutionalized for centuries in the United States (1972, p. 19). One might classify truth, goodness, and beauty as images that by custom are associated with white people, but not with black people in this country. This is a customary way of thinking about people who are white. But some of us know that some black people are truthful, good, and beautiful, too. By and large, these images of whites have been perpetuated by our institutional ways of describing people, places, and things. The association of whiteness with goodness or righteousness is a public point of view: innocent mistatements are called white lies while deceptive trickery is called black magic.

What are people who are black to do if they wish to be thought of as truthful, good, and beautiful? Because language is a means of influencing the inner world of all people, there was nothing left for blacks to do but to go on the offensive and to attack the public definition of that which was associated with truth, goodness, and beauty. The attack by blacks was direct. The phrase "Black is beautiful" that emerged during the civil rights movement of the mid-twentieth century in America was the attack. The designation of black as beautiful was an onslaught on the institutionalized practice mentioned above. Names, concepts, and images of language have been used to build up one group and by implication to put down another.

The black-is-beautiful language offensive has had some of the same negative side effects as the white-is-wonderful image. By implication, it excludes all who are not of the designated group. For this reason, the black-is-beautiful campaign has had only limited success largely because it is not an inclusive approach and also because there is so little positive reinforcement of blackness in our society. Most of the images customarily associated with it are bad. For example, the Macmillan guidelines state that "we have been trained to transform ordinary words into negative concepts, merely by adding 'black' to them: 'black market,' 'black sheep,' 'black day.' " The committee concluded, "It is understandable . . . that at an early age children begin to associate blackness with something undesirable and eventually transfer this response to people" (1975, p. 43). The Macmillan guidelines advise authors to "be sensitive to the use of the word 'black' and search for fresh expressions to counter negative meanings." The guidelines also urge authors to "reinforce positive attitudes toward blackness. For example, describe the appearance of black persons in terms of their 'soft black skin, sensitive black eyes, slender black hands, abundant black hair,' etc. instead of using stereotyped descriptions . . . " (Committee 1975, p. 43).

With reference to sexism in our writing, the guidelines state that "humanity" is an excellent concept that may be used in place of "mankind." Indeed, it is a more accurate description of a population consisting of men and women. When referring to a married couple, "husband and wife" is a better description than "man and wife." Those who were the architects of our present social system are our "forefathers," but there were women present at the beginning too. They should not be ignored. Thus, the guidelines indicate that "founders'" and "ancestors" are more appropriate nonsexist phrases that include the men and women who formed this nation. When describing an opinion that characterizes the rank and file, why not say it is the opinion of "the average person" rather than the opinion of "the man of the street" or "the man in the pew" (Committee 1975, pp. 18, 19, 20, 22).

Clearly the Macmillan guidelines intended to clarify rather than confuse and to make plain that which was confusing. One might expect writers who live by words such as James Kilpatrick, scholars, and all members of the knowledge industry to support rather than denounce such effort. A general theme of the Macmillan guidelines was that one should use a word that denotes inclusivity if one intends to be inclusive, and one should use a word that denotes exclusivity if one intends to be exclusive. As Joan Huber has put it, "To use 'men' to mean both 'men' and 'women and men' is an exercise in double-think" (1976, p. 89). We do not need this kind of thinking in this day and age that depends so heavily on accuracy and precision for our safety and security.

Probably more troubling to publishers than anything we have discussed thus far is the title to attach to women and the specific label for minorities in print. The guidelines offered this suggestion: "Use whichever title (Ms., Miss, or Mrs.) a woman prefers and . . . use Ms. or *no* title when preference is unknown" (Committee 1975, p. 20). With reference to race, the guidelines advise authors to avoid such labels as "colored people" or "Negroes," except when quoting another who has used these terms; the guidelines indicate that the most acceptable term is "black." "Native American" is offered as an alternative term for American Indian. The generic terms "Spanish-speaking Americans" or "Hispanic Americans" are acceptable, but specific designations, such as "Chicano" referring to the Mexican subculture in the United States are coming into use too. "Asian American" is a preferred generic term.

The new ways of labeling sex, race, and ethnic groups are in a state of flux and are troublesome to people in publishing. Publishing professionals, however, were not promised a rose garden when they came into the industry. Indeed one might classify the difficulty of determining how to label people an asset. It keeps one alert and in tune with the changing times.

There are two principles that should guide publishers' decisions regarding these matters. One has been mentioned already in the Macmillan guidelines: call people by the title or name that they prefer. The other: avoid using titles or names that simultaneously build up some people and put down others.

Titles of Women

Let us start with the first principle. A woman has a right to be called Miss, Mrs., or Ms. if she prefers to be recognized as Miss, Mrs., or Ms. To do otherwise is to cast doubt on the validity of an individual's preference in favor of that of a corporate practice when that individual's personal preference would do no harm to anyone. Institutions and corporations in our society exist for the sole purpose of enhancing individuals. Whenever individual and corporate preferences are in contention, individual preference always should take precedence if it is not harmful to others. I am aware of the fact that we have sacrificed individual interest to group or corporate interest for years in the United States, making this principle difficult to comprehend. Also, it is not possible in many instances to ascertain the title by which a person would like to be addressed when his or her name appears in print. Thus, the discussion that recommends a course of action of calling people by the title that they prefer when the opportunity to ask them is not available is somewhat academic. Moreover, there is a strong push toward uniformity in our modern urban technology-dominated society that is hard for most organizations to resist. Publishing is not exempted from the pressure toward uniformity and consistency.

The question, then, is how may publishers do that which is in their best interest without violating the self-interest of the person whose name appears in print. The answer to this question with reference to women raises several questions that should be on the policy agenda of all publishing corporations. First, why should anyone, male or female, black or white, be addressed by title in print? Second, if it is appropriate or necessary to identify people by title in print, why is a woman's relationship or function to a man a more important identifying characteristic of her being than her relationship to other categories of people? The title "Mister" does not indicate whether a man is single or married; and if he is married, it does not indicate whether he is living with his spouse, separated, divorced, or widowed. Why then should the title used to identify a woman reveal her marital status and, therefore, her function with reference to a man, when the reason for writing about her may not have anything to do with family life or heterosexual relations?

If "language [is] the circulation of meaningful interpretations carried by words through the stream of communications" (Benda 1961, p. 97), the continued acceptance by women of an identifying title that denotes their marital status is to accept the fact that their function with reference to men is the primary basis of their identity. Remember that words have no character in themselves but are conventional signs. Women have come to realize this and no longer wish to be assigned a function that may or may not be in their best interest. Some women resent the special sign of Miss and Mrs. that has been attached to them to signify the nature of their relationship with a man; others do not. For those who resent it, if there must be a title assigned to them for the sake of consistency and uniformity, call them Ms. For those who do not resent it, call them Miss or Mrs. if they prefer one of these signs. To repeat, when in doubt, call all women Ms. or call them by name only with no title attached.

Self-Designation of Blacks

The situation with blacks is the same. They too should have the privilege of a self-designated name. Any other approach is institutional arrogance. The name change by blacks has been a journey in search of an identity apart from the system that once demeaned them. During slavery they were called Negro, a name associated with negative images. Now they wish to be called black to separate themselves from vestiges of the past and all of its subservience and pain, especially the vestiges of slavery and the imagery that surrounded names in use at that time.

The early attempts at evolving a self-designated new name were quite modest. The NAACP led the fight and prodded newspapers and other publishing outlets to capitalize the "N" in Negro, presumably to indicate their status as a people. Even though W.E.B. DuBois, at the beginning of the twentieth century, observed that Negroes in America deserved a capital "N" for the word that designated them (DuBois 1900), it was not until the 1930s that such prestigious publications as the *New York Times* began to capitalize Negro. Volume I of *Southern History of the Civil War*, written by E.E. Pollard of Richmond, Virginia in 1863, identified "negro slavery" as the question that most seriously divided the country (1863, p. 3). Note the lower case "n" with which the term Negro was regularly written by whites during the nineteenth century and earlier.

Gaining a capital "N" to replace the lower case "n" in Negro was not enough. This did nothing to cast away the images of slavery attached to the name. So in an act of self-affirmation, Negroes decided to go for broke in their self-designation and named themselves *black*. Such a designation was a strange turn of events in view of the multiple negative images associated with black that were indicated earlier. Indeed, in some racially segregated communities, one of the most profane phrases that can be hurled at another is to call one a "black son of a bitch." A son of a bitch is not so bad, but a black son of a bitch is something terrible.

We can understand the appellation, black, as an honorable self-designation only by delving into history, on the one hand, and doing a bit of comparative analysis, on the other. At one period in the history of this nation some of the most professional and self-assured police chiefs wore small lapel pins that displayed the picture of a pig. During the late 1960s and early 1970s, pig was a derogatory name attached to the police by young radicals. If police officers could turn a symbol intended as an insult into a sign of jest, so can blacks.

By insisting that whites call them blacks, the former oppressed turned the tables on the former oppressors; the victimizers were met on their own turf. The victims were practicing moral alchemy that whites had practiced against blacks for years. Whatever was a virtue among whites in years gone by was designated as a vice when the same behavior appeared among blacks. For example, whites careful about the way they spent money were called thrifty, but blacks who were careful were called tight and stingy. Now that which was labeled a vice by the white outgroup (blackness and all of its negative images) was transformed by the Negro ingroup into a virtue (blackness as something beautiful). So virtuous is black from the point of view of the Negro moral alchemists that it no longer is a characteristic of their personhood but is of their essence. Thus most people who once called themselves Negroes now designate themselves as blacks. If that is what they wish to be called, that is what they ought to be called. It is a way of honoring individuals to call them what they wish to be called.

A brief historical perspective might be helpful. Hans Fantel in his book *Four-Letter Word Games* (1967) states that:

> To the theologically oriented . . . Lucifer, the embodiment of evil, is really a fallen angel. In short, that which is obscene . . . is at the same time that which—until relegated to hell—was sacred. . . .
>
> Obscenity grows from that which is holy and mysterious by an odd switch—throwing the original values in reverse.
>
> A case in point is that of the pig. Throughout the early cultures of the Near East, the pig was a sacred animal. As such, it was not eaten. Later on, when the Semites established domination of the area, they fashioned new myths and orthodoxies to bolster their territorial and political control. One of the basic techniques in the manufacture of new orthodoxies is to reverse earlier myths—as any propagandist knows. In this process of value reversal, the sacred pig became the dirty, unkosher pig. . . .
>
> While the social history of the pig . . . shows a value transformation from sacred to obscene . . . under certain conditions the practice of what is normally regarded as obscene becomes a sacred act (Fantel 1967, pp. 94-96).

Finally we face the issue of whether the "b" in black should be capitalized or written in a lower-case form. Earlier, civil rights organizations had insisted that the "n" in Negro should be capitalized. *Negro* presented as a proper noun recognized those to whom it referred to as "a people" with a specific place of origin. In the United States, Negro is a name for the people whose ancestors originated in Africa south of the Sahara. According to *The New Columbia Encyclopedia*, "The exploration of the African coast by Portuguese navigators resulted in the exploitation of the African as a slave and for nearly five centuries the predation of slave raiders along the coasts of Africa were to be a lucrative and important business conducted with appalling brutality" (*The New Columbia Encyclopedia* 1975, p. 2534). As early as 1440 Africans were brought to Portugal, which thus became "the first European country to engage in the African slave trade" (Franklin 1974, pp. 37-38).

Negro then refers to all people whose ancestors originated in a specific region of Africa. *Black* refers to all whose ancestors are of dark brown or ebony hue and, thus, is not limited to the people of a particular place. Negroes in the New World are a people because of their common experience of oppression solely because of their common ancestry. On a worldwide basis today, blacks have disparate experiences: some dominant and powerful, others subservient; some wealthy, others poor; some free, others enslaved. There is no common experience that characterizes all blacks. They, like whites, have many different experiences depending on the setting or system in which they live.

It is harder now to conceive of all blacks as a people and to describe them by a proper noun as a people. Nevertheless, racism still is rampant throughout the world and a case can be made that blacks are more frequently oppressed by whites and, therefore, continue to share this common existence despite the different settings and systems in which they are involved. So it is not entirely inappropriate to conceive of blacks as a people in comparison with whites and to designate the appellation identifying them as a proper noun. When this is done, however, the principle of equity should be invoked: the "w" in white should be capitalized so that it also stands as a proper noun. To do otherwise would violate the principle that one should avoid using titles or names that simultaneously build up some people and put down others.

In general, the color of a population should be considered as one of its several characteristics and not its essence. Thus, my preference is to write black and white with lower-case letters in the same manner that I describe male and female characteristics of populations, although I have not always followed my own advice. In the preface to *Racism and Mental Health* (Willie, Kramer, and Brown 1973, p. xv), the coeditors said, " . . . in the text Black and White are begun with capital letters. We assume that Black is customarily capitalized to indicate the status of Black individuals as a people. Noting how fine and beautiful peoplehood is for Blacks, the editors have recognized the peoplehood status for Whites, too, and thus have capitalized White." (Capitalizing black and white was a political act as well as a literary policy for the volume on *Racism and Mental Health*, which contained contributions from a range of specialists with disparate orientations on race. All did not agree to this style.) One cannot refer to the two groups in another way and be fair. Four alternatives are available for name calling with reference to populations classified by color: Black and White, Black and white, black and White, black and white. Only the first and the last are equitable and fair. All should be careful that their language signs and symbols are not used to build up one group and by implication put down another. Whether directed against blacks or whites, a putdown is unkind.

Institutional Oppression

What we have witnessed within a short period of time is the making of a new myth through the process of value reversal, that is, transforming black from that which is negative, terrible, and bad to that which is fine and beautiful. It would be immoral for any publisher to interfere with this transformation in the name of language purtiy and editorial continuity because of the dehumanizing consequence of the old myth.

There could be no better example of institutional racism than to insist that blacks be called Negroes and continue to function as in the past. The iconoclasts must have their way as they evolve new myths for a new day. Myth making is a tricky thing. Remember, an angel can become the devil, and black can become beautiful.

This has been a discussion about labeling and name calling. It is not definitive and cannot be, because the names and labels by which women and minorities call themselves and wish to be called are changing. It does not yet appear what the ultimate outcome will be. We see through a glass dimly some images of the future now. These we have analyzed and discussed. One thing is certain: middle-class, middle-aged men no longer may exercise the exclusive prerogative of labeling women and minorities as they wish. We now know that a name is more than a name; it also implies a function. Minorities and women are proceeding to name themselves. Wise are we who adopt their preferences in our books and other educational materials.

It is important to understand this discussion of group names, labels, and stereotypes not merely as a treatise on the proper usage of words but also as an analysis of the instruments of institutional oppression. The activity of naming a person, place, or thing is one way of exercising control over that which is named. A name has two properties—its denotation and its connotation. To denote a person, place, or thing is to mark off as one class or category and separate from others. To connote a person, place, or thing is to assess the unique qualities of the class or category, including its meaning and significance to others.

If the words used to classify also signify the significance of a person, place, or thing to others, then name calling can be a form of institutional oppression. Institutional oppression has to do with the structure and function of organizations rather than the attitude and behavior of individuals. Institutional oppression such as sexism or racism exists when the opportunities, obligations, and behavior of the people of one class or category are limited in a way that is inequitable and unfair in comparison with the people of other classes or categories.

If the denotation and connotation of a name imply a superior or inferior function, then the name itself contributes to oppression even though the people who use the name may not have intended such an outcome. It is important to realize that institutional oppression can be the unintended outcome of behavior thought even to be helpful. Thus, institutional oppression has to do with the effect of social action rather than with the intent. In

terms of effect, group names, labels, and stereotypes may qualify as a form
of institutional oppression.

References

Amory, Cleveland. 1960. *Who Killed Society?* New York: Harper & Row.

Arnez, Nancy L. 1972. "Enhancing the Black Self-Concept through Literature." In *Black Self-Concept*, edited by J.A. Banks and J.D. Grambs.
New York: McGraw-Hill.

Benda, Clemens. 1961. *The Image of Love*. New York: Columbia University Press.

Beuf, Ann H. 1977. *Red Children in White America*. Philadelphia: University of Pennsylvania Press.

The New Columbia Encyclopedia. Fourth Edition. 1975. New York: Columbia University Press.

Committee for Creating Positive Sexual and Racial Images in Educational
Materials. 1975. *Guidelines for Creating Positive Sexual and Racial Images in Educational Materials*. New York: Macmillan.

DuBois, W.E.B. 1900. *The Philadelphia Negro*. Philadelphia: Ginn.

Fantel, Hans. 1967. *Four-Letter Word Games*. New York: Evans.

Franklin, John Hope. Fourth Edition. 1974. *From Slavery to Freedom*.
New York: Knopf.

Greenough, James B., and Kittredge, George L. 1962. *Words and Their
Ways in English Speech*. Boston: Beacon Press.

Grimshaw, Allen. 1976. "The Editor's Page." *The American Sociologist*
2 (May): inside front cover.

Hernandez, Susan. 1976. "And Some Are More Equal Than Others." *The
American Sociologist* 2 (May):85-95.

Huber, Joan. 1976. "And Some Are More Equal Than Others." *The American Sociologist* 2 (May):85-95.

Kilpatrick, James J. 1976. "And Some Are More Equal Than Others."
The American Sociologist 2 (May):85-95.

Locke, Alain, and Stern, Bernard. 1942. "Types of Social Cleavage." In
When Peoples Meet. New York: Progressive Education Association.

Merton, Robert K. 1972. "Insiders and Outsiders: A Chapter in the Sociology of Knowledge." *American Journal of Sociology* 78 (July):9-47.

Monro, John U. 1978. "Teaching and Learning English." In *Black Colleges in America*, edited by Charles V. Willie and R.E. Edmonds. New
York: Teachers College Press.

Pollard, E.A. 1863. *Southern History of the Civil War*. Vol. 1. New York:
The Blue and Grey Press.

Willie, Charles V. 1972. *Black Students at White Colleges*. New York:
Praeger.

_____ . 1976. "And Some Are More Equal Than Others." *The American Sociologist* 2 (May):85-95.

Willie, Charles V., and Edmonds, R.E. eds. 1978. *Black Colleges in America*. New York: Teachers College Press.

Willie, Charles V.; Kramer, Bernard; and Brown, Bertram. 1973. *Racism and Mental Health*. Pittsburgh: University of Pittsburgh Press.

**Part VI
Administrative Issues and
Actions: Internal and External
Concerns**

14 Developing a Sense of Community on Campus: The Goal of Student Personnel Administrators

In the evolution of student personnel administration as a specialty in higher education, it is becoming increasingly common to classify student personnel workers as educators. This is as it should be, for the primary business of a college or university is formal education. All that is done on a campus should be for the purpose ultimately of enhancing the educational experience.

Yet after boldly asserting that they too should be called educators along with faculty members, student personnel workers tend to shy away from frank involvement in formal education. Some have said that their concern is with "the second curriculum"; by that they mean that all student activities, including those outside the classroom, should be learning experiences. Symbolic of this new thrust is the name change of dormitories to residence halls (Johnson 1970, p. 10) or living-learning centers.

Despite their assertion that they are educators, many student personnel administrators are reluctant to participate in the formal education of students in courses of instruction. There is a role for student personnel workers in formal education and ways in which contributions can be made both inside and outside the classroom. It is not enough, for example, to redefine counseling from "advice-giving" or "information-dispensing" to helping students acquire "self-understanding and insight" (Johnson 1970, p. 10). Student personnel workers ought to be directly involved in formal education as a way of enabling the college or university to achieve a sense of community.

Affective Participation

Courses taught by student personnel staff should focus on affective participation of students in the college or university community. Students perform a variety of roles having to do with leadership and friendship. Students, like other participants in the campus community, have instrumental and affective role relationships. Seldom do they receive any training for affective roles.

Student government leaders who work on behalf of a heterogeneous constituency can be effective only if they know how to achieve consensus and to negotiate for the fulfillment of student interests with administrators and faculty members. Moreover, the responsibility of allocating and supervising the expenditure of large sums of money collected from the student activity fee is devolved upon student leaders, and this is usually the first time in their lives that these students have assumed such a financial responsibility. On many campuses student leaders must coordinate a campus population sufficiently large to be classified as a small urban community. Most student leaders have to face these challenges and deal with them as best they can by trial and error. With little or no coaching available, the opportunity to learn about democracy in a real and living way is lost as students struggle for dominance and survival among themselves, sometimes using methods more appropriate for the nonhuman animal kingdom.

A formal course on campus organizations and decision making might be taught for student leaders as one way of equipping them with information and insight to deal with their leadership responsibilities. Such a course at Syracuse University was an effective way of helping students fulfill their leadership obligation. In this course student leaders were introduced not only to other student leaders but to the staff of the Office of Student Affairs and to outstanding faculty and administrators on campus. The student personnel staff members said that they and the student leaders developed a more trusting relationship as a result of their association with each other in class. Moreover, the adversarial relationship that tends to characterize some student-administration encounters was reduced in the class setting, and a spillover effect extended beyond the class. Although hesitant about the motives of the administrator-teacher for organizing the course at the beginning of the semester, the students eventually dropped their protective shields and interacted with the instructors as partners with a common goal: the search for a better understanding of the college or university as a social institution. From time to time guest lecturers from the faculty and the administration were invited to the course to discuss a common topic such as university governance. These encounters had cognitive and affective outcomes for the students as well as for the faculty and administrators.

Essentially, the course on campus organizations and decision making was designed to enhance the capacity of students to perform instrumental roles as campus leaders. Also it was a bonafide way for student personnel staff to become involved in formal education as educators. Students need help in learning how to relate to groups of diversified human beings. Some experienced on campus, for the first time, sustained associations with a variety of different people beyond family members or residents of the same neighborhood.

Peer Group Learning

Most of our educational activity at the college or university level is concerned with cognitive learning. We teach about life. Our students acquire much cerebral knowledge in the humanities, in the social and behavioral sciences, in mathematics and the physical sciences, and in the life sciences.

There is very little education in college or university concerning how to work effectively with others. Huston Smith made a strong case for what he calls "peer group learning," in which students learn how to relate to other human beings as human beings rather than as things and learn what Martin Buber really meant by an I-Thou relationship. A direct quote from Smith: "We need wisdom. To this end we need knowledge that is established in life: connected with feelings, illuminating choices in touch with wills. This is not exactly what we now have" (1973, pp. 2-4, 8).

Despite the presence of organized student life in undergraduate and graduate associations, a considerable amount of estrangement exists between students in different racial, ethnic, and sexual groups. Black students at Syracuse University, for example, wanted a larger slice of the student activity fee for programming to accommodate their enlarged population on campus. The white students in power (only two blacks were Student Assembly legislators at that time) resisted the request.

Meanwhile, the blacks had obtained from the University two houses for their student activities: the Black Student Union and the Afro-American Cultural Center. The Puerto Rican Organization was without any housing facility for its activities and occupied only one room in the Black Student Union. When university administrators inquired if the blacks might be willing, in the spirit of magnaminity, to give up one of their units to the Puerto Ricans, they were informed that blacks had to have two houses, although the Puerto Ricans had none.

Then the Women's Collective demanded a house where women could gather among themselves to deal with their unique concerns, which were aggravated by a sexist society. To emphasize their need, the women stated that they deserved a house more than blacks or Puerto Ricans. University administrators moved ahead with dispatch to find a house for the Women's Collective, which was all white. This group was urged to make contact with black women to determine if they could unite to fight sexism together; facilities were too limited to provide separate houses for a White Women's Center, a Black Women's Center, and a Brown Women's Center. Despite the perils of sexism, racism won out and no union was effected between the black and the white women on campus.

Just as administrators were about to make a final assignment of a university-owned house to the Women's Collective, the Graduate Student Organization stepped forth and insisted that it was in need of a house and that the needs of graduate students should take priority over the needs of women. In fact the graduate students said that they ought to be given the house that had been promised to the women.

These events caused the university administrators to conclude that some students did not like other students and needed help in developing affective relationships.

Estrangement among students of different racial or cultural groups has been noted elsewhere. For example, Michael Lerner in a publication entitled "Respectable Bigotry" stated that "Racism and bigotry toward black people is frighteningly apparent at Yale" (1971, p. 93). In a survey of four colleges in upstate New York, one student declared: "I had to go to a white school to find out I was black" (Willie and McCord 1972, p. 5). Education ought to be concerned with feelings as well as with facts. The estrangement among student groups on the campuses of higher education institutions ought to be of vital concern as an educational issue. There is something wrong with an educational system that does not help people learn how to live and work together for their mutual benefit.

A college or university must be concerned with affective as well as with instrumental roles. It should prepare students to interact with each other and with other members in the campus community. Such training is beneficial for the present as well as for the future.

Encounter Courses

To deal with the estrangement among student groups, the Office of Student Affairs joined with the Division of Psychiatry of the Student Health Service of Syracuse University to develop an appropriate course entitled "Prejudice and Racism" and offered it for three hours of college credit. The course instructors were administrators in these two units and were trained in sociology and psychiatry. Students affiliated with different racial, religious, and ethnic groups were deliberately recruited to participate in the course. Also participating in the course were five members of the administrative staff along with twenty-five students.

The course used the methods of group therapy in which the data for discussion were the personal experiences of the participants. The seminar dealt with the nitty-gritty issues such as a fight between a white male and a black female student in a dining hall; the feelings of women about the men who authorized a security poster showing a woman with a padlock on her blue jeans near the genital area and the advice that students should lock up their valuables; interracial dating and courtship between persons of different backgrounds; the conflict between "straight" students and "counter-culture" students; issues of freedom and dependency between offspring and parents; and points of conflict among students, faculty, and administrators. Much was learned about tension on campus and how to resolve it in these weekly sessions. A side benefit of the course was the increased understanding that took place between students and staff. The discussions revealed that students tend to dehumanize faculty and administrators and look upon them as robots programmed to fulfill assigned roles. The interaction in the course was a step toward overcoming the tendency of students to stereotype faculty and staff.

Huston Smith, who has taught several courses like this one, reported these reactions of his students: "They were glad we used this approach and recommended it be continued." Compared with other humanities courses, Smith's students told him that they "enjoyed it more, were more interested in it, and learned more from it." Smith was quick to state that he had no illusion that these statistics were "clean." Nevertheless, he believes that the benefits were sufficiently great that "it might be ideal for each . . . undergraduate to carry one encounter course each term," along with traditional courses (Smith 1973, pp. 2-4, 8).

All of this is to say that colleges and universities should give more attention to the emotional growth and development of their students. Patrick Terenzini analyzed data collected in a study of Syracuse University students by the Institute for Community Psychology. He found that two-thirds of the students on campus were in a personal state of malaise. They experienced uncomfortable feelings described as "really down," "jumpy," "nervous," and "hassled" (Terenzini 1973, p. 4). Educators tend to ignore these feelings in their quest for cognitive learning by students. Yet these feelings may interfere with cognition as well as impair effective social relations.

Syracuse University administrators experimented with ways of introducing affective learning into the curriculum through a course that utilized methods that encouraged students to turn toward each other. This is an approach that student personnel workers are uniquely capable of facilitating; furthermore, it is of educational value.

By helping students to understand the college or university as an institution in society and the function of individuals and groups within the educational system and by focusing upon the affective aspects of learning, student personnel workers may make solid contributions as educators to higher education.

References

Johnson, Walter F. 1970. "Student Personnel Work in Higher Education: Philosophy and Framework." In *College Student Personnel: Readings and Bibliographies*, edited by Laurine E. Fitzgerald, Walter F. Johnson, and Willie Norris. Boston: Houghton Mifflin.

Lerner, Michael. 1971. "Respectable Bigotry." In *Sociology and Student Life: Toward a New Campus*, edited by Arthur B. Shostak. New York: McKay.

Smith, Huston, 1973. "Two Kinds of Teaching." *The Key Reporter* 38 (Summer).

Terenzini, Patrick. 1973. *Counseling at Syracuse University*. Syracuse, NY: Office of Student Affairs, Syracuse University.

Willie, Charles V., and McCord, Arlene Sakuma. 1972. *Black Students at White Colleges*. New York: Praeger.

15

A Note on the Ethical and Moral Responsibility of Harvard and Other Schools as Investors

The President and Fellows of Harvard College (also known as the Harvard Corporation) issued a statement on April 27, 1978 that discussed "Harvard's ethical responsibilities as an investor in American companies doing business in or with South Africa." The statement called the policies of the South African government "repugnant and inhumane" and described the South African situation as "tragic and deplorable." Moreover, it declared that "corporations have moral responsibilities that transcend traditional corporate objectives, especially where they participate in a social and economic system such as that of South Africa" (Harvard College 1978).

The President and Fellows of Harvard College made these observations on the basis of their findings that "South Africa is virtually the only country in the world where racial exploitation is institutionalized and blatantly enforced on a massive scale." Since the Soweto riots in June 1976, their statement said, several hundred protesters have been killed and thousands have been arrested. In summary, there is no democracy in South Africa, where the "government controlled by two million whites uses a variety of sophisticated methods to monitor and control the lives and activities of more than 20 million nonwhite persons who are barred from voting or owning land except in designated areas of the country" (Harvard College 1978).

The President and Fellows of Harvard College said that they would support petitions that request companies in which Harvard University has investments that do business in or with South Africa to withdraw when "the nature of the company's operation in South Africa is such that its continued presence promises to do more to strengthen the existing regime than . . . contribute . . . to the eventual destruction of apartheid." Among those activities that could contribute to the eventual destruction of apartheid are the "making of appropriate efforts to introduce progressive employment and social policies" (Harvard College, 1978).

Under the law, there is a limit to what American companies can do for blacks and other nonwhites in South Africa. The public laws of South Africa place limitations on the jobs available to nonwhites, permit the government to enforce the separation of work facilities by race, and authorize the government to require any company in that country to manufacture and deliver to the government any product determined to be essential to the national security. The existence of these public laws were made known to the President and Fellows of Harvard College in a report that was prepared by the University's Advisory Committee on Shareholder Responsibility.

The Harvard Corporation has indicated in its statement that any company that remains in South Africa should "provide improved opportunities and employment practices for its black and other nonwhite employees." The statement implied that to "remain under an apartheid regime simply because it is profitable to do so" is an unacceptable alternative if efforts to implement improved opportunities for blacks and other nonwhites are not undertaken too (Harvard College, 1978).

If American companies remained in South Africa and did that which the President and Fellows of Harvard College recommended, they would be in violation of South African law and, in effect, would be practicing subversion. Let us change the circumstances and place the setting in the United States. It would be abhorrent to this nation if South African industries that operate in the United States attempted to subvert the Civil Rights Act of 1964 and clauses of our Constitution that guarantee equal protection of the laws for all. If it is inappropriate for foreign companies to intervene in the internal affairs of the United States, it is inappropriate for American companies to intervene in the internal affairs of South Africa.

In the spirit of national integrity and self-determination, the people of South Africa must face each other and resolve their differences. The differences between whites and nonwhites in South Africa may be resolved by way of conflict or of cooperation. Whatever method is used should be based upon the decisions of those who live in that nation and not because of subversive efforts by American companies and foreign nationals.

The South African conflict and its resolution need not be similar to that experienced by the South and the North of the United States more than a century ago. Yet it could be similar. Great Britain for economic reasons almost intervened in the American Civil War on the side of the South. If it had, the war between the states may have ended sooner, but the inhumane and repugnant institution of slavery would have continued longer. In the spirit of self-determination, the people of the United States had to resolve their own conflict, which they did. The same must occur between the people of South Africa, devoid of foreign intervention.

Thus, the American presence in South Africa as a participant in the economy of that nation is on the terms of the South African government. Otherwise, the American presence is subversive. In terms of the integrity of a nation-state, subversive activity for or against apartheid is inappropriate when exercised by a foreign nation-state. Under these conditions, the only honorable action that remains for foreign nationals who find the policies of the government with which they must do business to be inhumane and repugnant is to withdraw and cease cooperating with such a government.

On the basis of information and evidence, South Africa under its present government deserves to be isolated from the international community of nation-states until it treats its white, black, and other citizens in humane ways. To acknowledge that the South African government is inhumane and to continue to do business in South Africa in conformity with the inhumane laws that are promulgated by that inhumane government is to place oneself in the intolerable situation of being an accomplice.

The President and Fellows of Harvard College said that "certain companies may play their most effective role by improving working conditions and opportunities for nonwhite workers and others should withdraw, either because they are unwilling or unable to introduce progressive employment or social practices or because the value of such practices is outweighed by the particular benefits their continued presence brings to the South African regime." The statement asserted that both approaches "can have a constructive influence" and concluded that, at least for the present, "no compelling reason has been shown for choosing one to the exclusion of the other" (Harvard College 1978).

I believe that the moral responsibility of the Harvard Corporation is a compelling reason for requesting all American companies in which it has investments to withdraw from South Africa. It is important to distinguish between morality and ethics in determining an appropriate course of action.

Ethical action involves making a proper estimation of others' needs and then acting on the basis of such information to fulfill those needs in ways that are fair to all participants. The Harvard Corporation has accepted the recommendation of its Advisory Committee on Shareholder Responsibility regarding the kinds of data that should be obtained in the future to make a proper estimation of the needs and activities of American companies in South Africa. Harvard already has obtained sufficient data to make a proper estimation of the needs and activities of the South African government and the whites it represents. Thus far, Harvard has not devised a way to obtain reliable information to make a proper estimation of the needs of blacks and other nonwhites in South Africa. This it must do as an ethical responsibility if companies in which the University has investments are encouraged to remain in South Africa and to act in ways that are fair to all, including nonwhites.

The statement of the President and Fellows of Harvard College acknowledged that "prominent black South Africans and many organizations have come out in favor of withdrawal." Then the statement attempted to balance that opinion with a quote from Percy Quoboza, a black South African editor and former Nieman Fellow, who urged United States corporations "to play a far more active role in helping to remove the walls of discrimination.'' The President and Fellows of Harvard College could have quoted from Stephen Biko, who told a white South African journalist, Donald Woods that ''the liberal is no enemy, he's a friend—but for the moment he holds us back, offering a formula too gentle, too inadequate for the struggle.'' Mr. Biko said to his white journalist friend that the Americans are nice enough people ''but their approach is doing us no damn good.'' Further, he said that if there is to be a peaceful solution in South Africa, the Americans ''must stop talking and start really getting tough—sanctions, blockades if necessary, the lot. We blacks reject the theory that sanctions will harm us more'' (quoted in Woods, 1979). Since making these statements, Biko was killed while in the custody of South African government officials.

I contend that opinions by South African blacks and other nonwhites are not perfectly balanced for and against the continued participation of American companies in the economy of that country and that the information we have is inadequate for making a proper estimation of the needs of South African nonwhites. The absence of such information and the failure to devise a procedure for obtaining it constitute a default of our ethical responsibility if a decision that supports American companies remaining in South Africa is intended to be fair to blacks, whites, and other people in that country. It is essential that the matter of adequate information regarding the needs of blacks and other nonwhites should be addressed in addition to devising procedures for obtaining better information from American companies, for the President and Fellows of Harvard College indicated that their concern is with ''Harvard's ethical responsibilities as an investor in American companies doing business in or with South Africa'' (Harvard College 1978).

Moral behavior has to do with what is right or wrong. The definition of right and wrong is a function of standards or values of a group or collectivity with which one identifies and to which one pledges allegiance. Harvard identifies with the United States which values democracy and promotes human rights as public policy. To support the South African government, actively or by acquiescence, and its laws that violate standards of democracy and decency is to engage in action that is wrong morally.

In determining the course of action for Harvard as an investor that is right morally, the issue of ''whether economic pressure resulting from withdrawal would push the government to relax apartheid or simply provoke more restrictive measures'' is irrelevant. The moral issue is whether it is right to do business with a government that oppresses its people. Morality is not concerned with making a proper estimation of another person's need and then attempting to fulfill the other's need in a way that is fair. Morality has to do with whether or not one's actions violate the standards of the group with which one identifies. Morality and ethics are linked, however. It would appear to be unfair to require an individual who is attempting to fulfill his or her ethical responsibility by attending to another's need to do this by violating the standards and values of his or her own group.

The President and Fellows of Harvard College have expressed uncertainty concerning whether remaining or withdrawing will eventually prove most effective in bringing an end to apartheid in South Africa. Although the ethical responsibility may be unclear for the present, the President and Fellows of Harvard College have made a decisive judgment about the immorality of the South African government with reference to standards of democracy and decency. As Harvard's ethical responsibility as an investor in companies that do business in South Africa becomes clear in the years ahead, it is inconceivable that this responsibility would require violation of Harvard's moral responsibility.

In the absence of a clear concept of what should be done ethically, Harvard and other institutions are left with but one alternative, and that is to do what is right and responsible morally.

The operations of Eastman Kodak Company in South Africa were examined, as a typical example, to determine the extent to which they conform to the Harvard guidelines. The chairman of the board of Kodak informed the 1978 annual meeting of the stockholders that Kodak will sell products around the world within the laws and regulations of the U.S. government (Eastman Kodak Company 1978, p. 18). My inquiry was how Kodak could conform to the U.S. Civil Rights Act of 1964, which prohibits discrimination by race, when the laws of South Africa require segregation and discrimination by race.

To undertake the analysis I requested information on company policy and practice pertaining to the treatment of Kodak's employees in South Africa. The Harvard guideline stated that companies in which the university is an investor should adopt a policy of treating all employees fairly and should follow the practice of increasing opportunities for blacks in South Africa (Harvard College 1978).

The "Report on Kodak in South Africa" that was prepared by the company in December 1977 stated that the "uncertainties" in South Africa because of the "increasing strain" of the "political, social, and economic fabric" of that country have had "an adverse effect on Kodak's business" there. The report acknowledged that "the root source of South Africa's social and economic problems lies in the system of apartheid" and said that "Kodak's best interest would not be served by . . . expansion of production facilities in South Africa." The report explained that "Kodak's practice" is "to live within the law in all countries where its facilities are located" and stated that "several South African laws affect Kodak employment practices" (Eastman Kodak Company Report 1977).

The corporation secretary of the Eastman Kodak Company stated that the U.S. Civil Rights Act of 1964 is not applicable to Kodak's operations outside the United States and its possessions but that the company does obey United States law and regulations that govern business with other nations such as the U.S. Commerce Department regulation of February 1978 that bans sales to or for the use of the South African military or police. Moreover, he said, Kodak is firmly committed to a policy of nondiscrimination in South Africa and to furthering the well-being of its employees in that country. The corporation secretary presented this information to me in a personal letter dated July 31, 1978.

Despite the Kodak policy, the company practice in South Africa revealed a disproportionate effort in providing employment opportunities for white as compared with black and colored employees. The company prepared report on Kodak in South Africa (1977) indicated that Kodak had a staff of 470 employees in South Africa in 1977, of whom 101 were black and 140, colored. Thus, nearly half the company's employees were white, despite the fact that whites constituted only about one-sixth of that nation's population. Of the 241 black and colored employees of Kodak in South Africa in 1977, only 2 were supervisors and 1 a supervisor trainee.

Despite the company's claim that "the main reason for the absence of many Blacks [in] higher level jobs is the inadequate quality of education and training they have received prior to entering industry," the company benefit program that provided educational assistance for the education of South African employees assisted only 6 employees in 1977, and all 6 were white (Eastman Kodak Company Report 1977).

In the year preceding 1977, Kodak in South Africa provided specialized educational training to 164 workers, of whom 37 were colored and 12, black. During the same period, supervisory training was provided by the company for about 100 workers, but only 18 of this number were either black or colored (Eastman Kodak Company Report 1977).

According to data prepared by Kodak, the system of apartheid has strained the political, social, and economic fabric of South Africa and has had an adverse effect on Kodak's business in South Africa. Clearly Kodak's operations in South Africa are not contributing to the destruction of apartheid as called for in the Harvard guideline: a corporate officer has said that it is company policy to obey the laws of host countries. Clearly Kodak operations in South Africa have not significantly improved working conditions and opportunities for nonwhite workers as called for in the Harvard guidelines. A disproportionately large number of its South African employees are white; the number of black and colored workers who have received company initiated supervisory and other special training is disproportionately small.

In light of the fact that the strained political, social, and economic fabric of South Africa is directly associated with its system of apartheid and that this situation has had an adverse effect on Kodak's business in that country, one wonders why the industry does not withdraw. Kodak's company policy is to abide by the laws of host countries, and public laws in South Africa support the segregation and oppression of nonwhites. A corporate officer of the company responded to this question by stating that Kodak had a commitment to its employees in South Africa and intended to stay and work for constructive change even though the company claims that it has only 20 percent of the photographic business in South Africa. He did not indicate how an industry could foster constructive change and at the same time obey racist laws. The "Report on Kodak in South Africa" has demonstrated that efforts thus far have been ineffective in providing equal employment opportunities for an appropriate number of blacks and coloreds in that country.

This analysis and these conclusions were shared with the Eastman Kodak Company through the office of the Chairman of the Board and with Harvard University through the offices of the president and of the Advisory Committee on Shareholder Responsibility.

Given the set of circumstances discussed above, some colleges and universities have decided that the only moral, ethical, or legal alternative is to divest. For example, the University of Wisconsin in 1978 sold more than $9 million in stocks and bonds that represented South Africa ties, according to the *Milwaukee Journal* (1978, p. 13). This action was taken in accordance with a resolution of the board of regents to divest the University of Wisconsin of investments in firms doing business in South Africa. Because of the volatile nature of the stock market, the University of Wisconsin received five hundred forty thousand dollars less than it originally had paid for the stocks and bonds. However, the Wisconsin attorney general said that the divestment was necessary because the investment violated a state law prohibiting the University of Wisconsin from investing in firms that discriminate.

Harvard University in 1981 "sold fifty million dollars in Citibank notes and certificates of deposit that had been part of its investment portfolio" because of Citibank's participation in a loan by Swiss, French, and German banks to the South African government that was at odds with Harvard's policy adopted in 1978. That policy forbids Harvard "from keeping its money in banks . . . that make loans to the apartheid-supporting government of South Africa" (*Boston Globe*, 1981, p. 57).

The president of Harvard University said that although it would cost the university a "considerable amount of money" to divest itself of holdings in corporations doing business in South Africa, the potential loss is not the only reason the corporation is opposed to immediate divestiture of all investments in companies in South Africa (*Harvard Crimson* 1978, p. 1).

However, the financial sacrifice has factored into the decision of some colleges and universities not to divest. A Syracuse University vice president said that "apartheid is morally repugnant" but that his school would pay between one hundred fifty thousand dollars and two hundred thousand dollars in commission fees to sell the stock of companies with holdings in South Africa and replace them with other stock. The university officer questioned whether such an expenditure for the purpose of divestiture because of the racial policies of South Africa would violate the legal requirement to manage an institution's portfolio in a "prudent" manner (*Syracuse New Times* 1979, p. 6). The president of Harvard said that "the Corporation decided that it could achieve more by shareholder pressure than [by] 'a single dramatic act of divestiture' " (*Harvard Crimson* 1978, p. 1). Similar sentiments were expressed by some other schools such as Syracuse University, whose vice president for public affairs said that "it would be wiser to keep the stock, thereby retaining the power to vote on company policy resolutions at stockholder meetings" (*Syracuse New Times* 1979, p. 6).

However, corporate actions of several colleges and universities have not been consistent with the attitudes expressed by their officers. For example, in 1978, Syracuse University "abstained from voting on a proposal that would require Eastman Kodak Company to not make or renew any contracts or agreements to sell photographic equipment to the South African government" (*Syracuse New Times* 1979, p. 6). Despite the earlier mentioned poor record of Kodak in upgrading black and colored employees in South Africa, and despite the fact that photographic equipment can be used to make identity cards for nonwhites that enable the government severely to restrict their mobility, a major university refused to take action for or against an alleged commercial practice that could have an adverse effect on the South African black population. Such inaction would appear to be a failure to act responsibly as a shareholder. Yet the possibility of pressuring industries to act in ways that would foster human dignity in South Africa is one reason given by many educational institutions for not divesting. An inconsistency is revealed regarding institutional principle and institutional practice.

By refusing to divest, or to force industries in which one is a stockholder to change practices that contribute to oppression in South Africa, or to encourage American companies to withdraw from the South African market, American colleges and universities risk the loss of some of their moral capital in the long run for the sake of holding onto limited financial capital in the short run.

Several years ago Benjamin Mays, who was president of Morehouse College during the 1940s, 1950s, and part of the 1960s, said that belief is the basis of action and that one who does not act on the basis of belief has no belief at all but merely an opinion. Harvard University, Syracuse University, and other colleges and universities have stated that apartheid is repugnant. If this is their belief, the colleges and universities of this nation ought to be prepared to act affirmatively; otherwise, they merely have an opinion about the immorality of apartheid and not a belief. To attempt to act in a moral way as an institution may raise troublesome questions. But having a belief and failing to act in accordance with it in the end may be even more troublesome if one is an educational institution and if education is understood as a means of liberation.

References

Boston Globe. 1981. 19 February. "Harvard Sells Securities to Protest Citibank Loan."

Eastman Kodak Company. 1977. "Report on Kodak in South Africa." December.

———. 1978. Corporation Secretary's personal communication to Charles V. Willie. 31 July.

Harvard College, President and Fellows. 1978. Statement. Cambridge, Mass., 27 April.

Harvard Crimson. 1978. 1 May.

Milwaukee Journal. 1978. 26 July.

Syracuse New Times. 1979. 9 May.

Woods, Donald. 1979. *Biko*. New York: Random House.

16 A Tribute to Benjamin Elijah Mays: Master Teacher and Administrator

The Morehouse College that Benjamin E. Mays and others helped to build has served higher education well by demonstrating how to unite the method of education with the purpose of education. By so doing, it produced a prophet, a twentieth century suffering servant, and a national redeemer in its son Martin Luther King, Jr, whose spirit death could not swallow up. The death of Martin Luther King, Jr. was a full, perfect, and sufficient sacrifice for the redemption of America from racism. Benjamin Mays was King's mentor. King was a member of the class of 1948 and, as stated before, the most famous graduate of this college that is more than a century old.

Samuel DuBois Cook, King's classmate at Morehouse College and in 1976 president of Dillard University, came to Cambridge, Massachusetts to celebrate the nation's bicentennial year and left these words echoing in the halls of Harvard: Martin Luther King, Jr., Cook said, had to graduate from Morehouse Colege rather than from Harvard College. This is what I think he meant. At Morehouse College, King, Cook, and others learned that law and order, a method of social organization, is demonic unless it occurs within the context of love and justice, the purpose of social organization. Method and purpose complement each other and ought always to be kept together in higher education as well as in public affairs. The Morehouse College that King knew was fashioned in the image of Mays: it united principle and practice, idea and action, words and works. Because at Morehouse College there was no separation between law and order and love and justice, its graduates have seen and experienced how these ideals work together and have insisted that the United States unite them so that the races of this nation may be reconciled.

The Civil Rights Act of 1964 and the Voting Rights Act of 1965 were the handiwork of Martin Luther King, Jr., the President and Congress of the United States, and liberated blacks and whites, according to President Jimmy Carter, an honorary alumnus of Morehouse College. Students and graduates of Morehouse were deeply involved in all aspects of the civil rights movement.

My main criticism of many predominantly white and predominantly black colleges and universities is that they have permitted the dual perspective to separate. Predominantly white colleges, for example, have focused on methods of knowing, almost to the exclusion of any consideration of the purpose of knowledge. Despite our national high rate of literacy and the large amount of funds invested in higher education, our society still has not affirmed that all human beings are sacred and significant. Many of the students at the prestigious research colleges and universities of this nation are preoccupied with the mathematical and exponential methods of the natural sciences, the quantitative and other forms of analysis of the social sciences, the techniques of design and form in music and art, and methods of logic and criticism in philosophy and literature. Learning experiences that deal with suffering, sacrifice, service, and our purpose and mission in life are not on the educational agendas of many predominantly white colleges.

Many students in the relatively small predominantly black colleges are preoccupied with the purpose of being, almost to the exclusion of any concern about methods and techniques of validating knowledge. It is fair to say that black and other minority students have been on an identity binge. They have been grappling with the questions of purpose: Who am I? Why am I here? What is my mission? With whom must I accomplish this mission? Learning experiences in logic, statistics, qualitative forms of analysis, techniques of evaluation, and the testing and measuring of validity and reliability are not on the educational agendas of some college students who attend predominantly black colleges. Courses in these areas have to do with methods of knowing. Racial minority students are preoccupied with purpose.

Out of Epworth, South Carolina came Benjamin E. Mays to bridge the void between higher education as method and as purpose. During the twenty-seven years of his administration at Morehouse, Mays accomplished what many in higher education had failed to do: he united purpose with method. Because of this union, education at Morehouse had a profound impact on Martin Luther King, Jr., who at the end of his mission said, "a true hybrid, a combination of two cultures, . . . offers the best answer to many of life's dilemmas" (King 1968, p. 61).

In the concluding chapter of *Black Colleges in America*, a book that is based on presentations at the Black College Conference at Harvard University, I tried to explain how Mays united two cultures, why Mays was the messenger of reconciliation, how Mays achieved the rapprochement between purpose and method in higher education that had drifted apart. My conclusion is that he was able to do this because Mays was a marginal man, one who has lived in, between, and beyond his race and his region as discussed in chapter 2. Reconciling opposites was a way of life for him.

Robert Park of the University of Chicago, who wrote about the marginal person in the 1930s, said that "[he or she] is always relatively the more civilized human being." The marginal person is "the individual with the wider horizon, the keener intelligence, the more detached and rational viewpoint." In the past, we have looked upon marginal people as neither fish nor fowl; they are those who fall between the cracks. But I see a new concept of the marginal person based on Park's analysis. The marginal person also is one who rises above two social or cultural groups, freeing the different people to work together (Stonequist 1937, p. xviii). Everett Stonequist, a student of Park, had some appreciation of the value and utility of this role. He described the marginal person as "the key-personality in the contact of cultures. It is in his [or her] mind that the cultures come together, conflict, and eventually work out some kind of mutual adjustment." Endorsing Park's view that marginal people always are the relatively more civilized human beings, Stonequist concluded that "the life histories of marginal [people] offer the most significant material for the analysis of the cultural process" (1937, p. 222). The life history of Benjamin Elijah Mays, a marginal man, offers the most significant material for the analysis of the true function of higher education in America (see Mays 1971).

In his personhood, Mays united black and white colleges, spending one year at Virginia Union University in the South and the remainder of his college and postgraduate years at Bates College and the University of Chicago in the North. As a Pullman porter as well as a college teacher, Mays in his adult years performed both blue-collar and white-collar work. As a teacher of mathematics, English, and religion, Mays united science and the humanities. As a college professor and a college president, Mays followed an academic career of teaching and research as well as of administration. He was a marginal man who brought unity out of diversity.

The life of Benjamin E. Mays was complex and full of contrasts. His genius was a capacity to synthesize opposites and apparent contradictions into a new harmonic whole. As an educator, Mays pioneered in fashioning the Morehouse College campus into a just community long before courses in moral education were fashionable listings in other college catalogues. There was student participation on Morehouse College committees during his administration long before there were student demonstrations to achieve this goal at other schools. Mays knew that his students were youthful, but he treated them as gentlemen and insisted that their arguments be logical and that they be personally accountable for their behavior.

In a meeting of Baptist lay people and clergy, Mays said, "It is my considered judgment that Martin Luther King, Jr., had to come out of Morehouse." It is my considered judgment that Morehouse College as an institution of higher education that united method and purpose had to spring forth from Benjamin Mays, a man of big ideas who dealt with details, a philosopher and theoretician with a pragmatic approach. For these reasons it was the unanimous decision of the staff of the Black College Conference at Harvard University that our book on *Black Colleges in America* should be dedicated to our teacher, preacher, president, and politician—Benjamin Elijah Mays, a legend in his own time.

References

King, Martin Luther, Jr. 1968. *Where Do We Go From Here: Chaos or Community?* New York: Harper & Row (hardcover). Boston: Beacon Press, (paperback).

Mays, Benjamin E. 1971. *Born to Rebel.* New York: Scribner's.

Stonequist, Everett V. 1937. *The Marginal Man.* New York: Scribner's.

Willie, Charles V., and Edmonds, R.E., eds. *Black Colleges in America.* New York: Teachers College Press.

Part VII
Concluding Statement

17 The Future of Desegregated Higher Education

The *Sweatt* and *McLaurin* cases in Texas and Oklahoma anticipated the *Brown* ruling. They required stated government to equalize educational opportunities in higher education with reference to buildings, curricula, salaries of teachers, and other tangible factors (*Sweatt* v. *Painter* 1950; *McLaurin* v. *Oklahoma State Regents* 1950). Just as these cases laid a foundation for the *Brown* decision, so the *Brown* and *Adams* cases have become a foundation for litigation with reference to other forms of state sanctioned inequality.

If education is for the purpose of equipping people with knowledge and virtue to manage the society, then it is almost impossible to justify excluding anyone from the opportunity to receive an education, for ignorance harms not only the individual but the total society. The growing movement to overcome inequality of opportunity because of race now encompasses age, sex, physical or mental status, and eventually will include social class or wealth.

Langdon Gilkey, a United States citizen who saw people stripped bare of pretensions in an internment camp of two thousand women, men, and children that was located in Asia during World War II, kept a rather lengthy journal and formed this opinion about the moral basis of knowledge and rationality: "Rational behavior in communal action is primarily a moral and not an intellectual achievement, possible only to a person who is morally capable of self-sacrifice. In a real sense . . . moral selflessness is a prerequisite for the life of reason—not its consequences" (Gilkey 1966, p. 93). His elaboration of this idea brings the issue of the purpose of education into perspective.

> Technological advance . . . spells "progress" only if [people] are in fact rational and good. A [person] motivated only by self-interest, a [person] subject to brutal or vicious prejudices and passions, one who can kill and maim with ease if [one's] security is threatened, is no technologist in whom to have confidence. . . . A realistic view of [people] tends to undermine the confidence a technological culture has in its own progress. Since we all want to believe in something, our secularized culture has tended to adopt an idealistic view of [people] as innately rational and good, as able to handle [themselves] and [their] own history with the relative ease with which [they] dealt with nature. Consequently, the scientist rather than the politician, the knower rather than the moralist, has seemed to us to be the guarantor of security and peace, the harbinger of a better world.

As I learned in camp, this vision is a false dream: the things we long
for—peace, prosperity, and a long life—depend to a far greater degree on
the achievement of harmony and justice among [people] than they do on
the latest inventions from our laboratories, valuable as the latter may be.
That achievement of harmony and justice confronts us as a race, not with
problems of technological know-how or scientific knowledge so much as
with the problems of political and moral decisions (Gilkey 1966, pp. 95-96).

The wisdom of Langdon Gilkey that was derived from his prison camp
experience indicates that our current emphasis on knowledge, information,
and individual achievement imbalances the purpose of education and may
even misdirect it. Thus, Daniel Bell's recommendation that "high-scoring
individuals [on the Intelligence Quotient scale] . . . should be brought to
the top in order to make the best use of their talents" should be rejected as
connoting a definition of education that is too limited (Bell 1973, p. 608).
"Rational behavior in communal action," as indicated by Gilkey, "is
primarily a moral and not an intellectual achievement." The most in-
telligent people may or may not be sufficiently selfless to make rational and
appropriate decisions for the public good. The purpose of education, then,
is to provide learning opportunities for the acquisition of knowledge and
wisdom for the making of political and moral decisions that sustain communal life.

This purpose has nothing to do with the notion of "equality of output"
as an educational goal that is discussed by James Coleman (1968, p. 106)
and Daniel Bell (1973, p. 620). What anyone achieves or produces because
of greater natural or cultivated capacities should work for the good of the
least fortunate, according to John Rawls (1971, pp. 302-303). Moreover, we
know that a heterogeneous population is better capable of exploiting an environment than one that is homogeneous. Why then should public policy
about education emphasize equal results when a polymorphic society of
people with different talents is better? It is equality of opportunity about
which desegregated higher educational policy should be concerned, not
equality of results.

Education in the future will be concerned about social class integration
as well as racial desegregation. Schools of pluralistic populations will have
new educational goals that emphasize truth and honesty as well as proficiency in communication and calculation skills. These changes will occur as
the minorities of this nation—blacks, the poor, Hispanics, Native
Americans, Asian Americans, and the physically handicapped—continue to
practice the grand tradition of serving as creative dissenters by insisting that
the United States live up to its basic constitutional values of freedom and
justice for all. Education in a setting of segregation fosters attitudes of en-
titlement and estrangement. This kind of education is deficient.

The liberation and reform of education today by the school desegregation court cases initiated by minorities is reminiscent of the way that societies have been renewed and regenerated in the past. Commenting on the role of minorities in the regeneration of human societies, Richard Korn has reminded us of the wisdom of Polybius that was expressed several centuries ago. In *The Histories*, book 57 (quoted in Korn 1968, pp. 195-196), Polybius said, "When a new generation arises and the democracy falls into the hands of the grandchildren of its founders, they have become so accustomed to freedom and equality that they no longer value them and begin to aim at pre-eminence." Korn's interpretation of this statement is that "the inheritors of greatness waste the heritage. The passive beneficiaries of liberty become oppressive." Then Korn asked this question: "Who is left to keep the flame alive—whence comes the regeneration?" His answer: regeneration of the system tends to come from the oppressed (Korn 1968, pp. 195-196).

In the *Brown* v. *Board of Education* decision of 1954, the U.S. Supreme Court described an equitable educational process as one in which a student of one racial group is able "to engage in discussion and exchange views with other students." Obviously, racial segregation prohibits this kind of exchange between racial minority and majority students so that the Court, therefore, declared it to be unlawful in public education.

Desegregated higher education is compassionate, recognizes individual differences, compensates for personal limitations so that all may participate in social organization as extensively as possible, and asks none to be more than he or she is capable of becoming but accepts each person for what one is, was, and hopes to be. In the future, learning not achievement will be recognized as the essence of education. Learning occurs in situations of failure as well as success. Learning is an activity that occurs in a relationship. It is process, not a product.

Equal educational opportunity means that each person is provided an opportunity to learn how to function in a way that fulfills his or her self-interests for the common good. This happens when society makes it possible for each person to become what one is capable of becoming. To date, few members of minority groups, socioeconomic, racial, or otherwise, have had the opportunity to become all that they are capable of being.

An educational goal that focuses on equal results will be renounced in the future as a relic of the elitist age of meritocracy that was sustained and supported by racial and social class segregation.

Desegregated higher education of the future will be education for life in a pluralistic society. Student bodies and faculties of colleges and universities will be diversified so that they will consist of a majority and various minorities, including those of various racial, ethnic, socioeconomic, handicapped, and age groups. Multicultural schools with diversified student bodies are of distinct educational benefit in eliminating intergroup stereotypes and in providing students with a reality that is similar to that found in the community at large.

Meyer Weinberg (1977, p. 11) has called segregated education "the system of compulsory ignorance." It should be obvious that such a system can have a negative effect upon white as well as black or other racial minority students, upon the affluent and the poor, and upon the healthy and the handicapped. Moreover, a segregated system of compulsory ignorance can breed inappropriate feelings of superiority and inferiority that are harmful to the majority as well as to the minority.

When people of varying status levels, for example, interact with each other in school over an extended period of time, the possibility is that they may learn from each other, trust each other, and become friends. Continuous dialogue and communication between the high and mighty and the meek and lowly tend to result in genuine caring across class and caste lines.

Because learning is the result of a relationship, the association among students of varying circumstances enriches their knowledge and wisdom. Such knowledge and wisdom are essential in managing a pluralistic society. This kind of learning is different from that obtained indirectly about people whom one has not seen, does not know, and cannot call by name. Desegregated higher education in the future will facilitate learning by direct contact with a wide range of people.

In one generation, the United States has experienced a major transformation with reference to education. In 1950, a few years before the Supreme Court rendered the historic *Brown* v. *Board of Education* decision, educational expenditures accounted for slightly more than 3 percent of the gross national product. As the 1980s began, the figure had more than doubled. In 1950, slightly more than 31 million individuals were enrolled in schools including elementary and secondary schools, colleges, and universities. During the bicentennial year, 1976, nearly 60 million persons were enrolled and were about equally divided between males and females.

An increasing number of high school graduates are receiving a college education. About three out of every ten people over twenty-five years of age have attended college (U.S. Bureau of Census 1978, pp. 131-172).

These facts indicate that more and more people probably will participate in postsecondary educational opportunities in the years to come. The trend of greater participation in postsecondary education by all sorts and conditions of people will diminish the elitist characteristic of a college degree. In the past, higher education has been looked upon as something exclusive largely because it has been limited to a relatively small proportion of the adult population. However, with an increase in the number of people who graduate from high school and go on to college, postsecondary institutions no longer will be able to hold to their current ideal of exclusivity. Already some educators are declaring that there is no such person as an unworthy seeker of knowledge. Desegregated education is demonstrating the value of this idea.

John Rawls described why equality of opportunity is necessary. He said, "No one deserves his greater natural capacity nor merits a more favorable starting place in society." Rawls approves of a social system (and presumably an educational system) in which "no one gains or loses from his arbitrary place in the distribution of national assets or his initial position in society without giving or receiving compensating advantages in return" (Rawls 1971, p. 101). This kind of society would be just and fair. It is the purpose of higher education to maintain and sustain such a society, and desegregation is a method for achieving this end.

References

Bell, Daniel. 1973. "On Meritocracy and Equality." In *Power and Ideology in Education*, edited by Jerome Karabel and A.H. Halsey, pp. 607-635. New York: Oxford University Press.

Brown v. *Board of Education of Topeka*. 1954. 347 U.S. 483.

Coleman, James S. 1968. "Equality of Educational Opportunity." *Integrated Education* 6, no. 5 (September-October).

Gilkey, Langdon. 1966. *Shantung Compound*. New York: Harper & Row.

Korn, Richard R., ed. 1968. *Juvenile Delinquency*. New York: Crowell.

McLaurin v. *Oklahoma State Regents*. 1950. 339 U.S. 637.

Rawls, John. 1971. *A Theory of Justice*. Cambridge, Mass.: Harvard University Press.

Sweatt v. *Painter*. 1950. 339 U.S. 629.

U.S. Bureau of the Census, 1978. *Statistical Abstract of the United States: 1978*. Washington, D.C.: U.S. Government Printing Office.

Weinberg, Meyer. 1977. *A Chance to Learn*. New York: Cambridge University Press.

Index

Index

About the Author

Charles Vert Willie, a sociologist, is professor of education and urban studies, Harvard University Graduate School of Education. Previously, he served as chairman of the Department of Sociology and vice president at Syracuse University. He received the Ph.D. degree from Syracuse University, and the B.A. and M.A. degrees from Morehouse College and Atlanta University.

A past president of the Eastern Sociological Society, Professor Willie has served on the governing council of the American Sociological Association, the Board of Directors of the Social Science Research Council, the President's Commission on Mental Health, and the Panel on the Benefits of Higher Education of the Board of Human Resources.

He has participated as a faculty member, administrator, and trustee of higher-education institutions for more than three decades. His teaching experience has varied from service in a college of arts and sciences, a medical center, and a theological seminary, to service in a school of education. His other books on higher education are *Black Students at White Colleges,* *Black Colleges in America,* and *The Sociology of Urban Education.*